1 0 STEPS

Successful Project Management

Lou Russell

If no CD-ROM is included with this book,
please go to www.astd.org/10StepsProjectManagement
to download the handouts and other materials to your hard drive.

P R E S S

Alexandria, Virginia

ASTD Press is an internationally renowned source of insightful and practical information on workplace learning and performance topics, including training basics, evaluation and return-on-investment (ROI), instructional systems development (ISD), e-learning, leadership, and career development.

Ordering information: Books published by ASTD Press can be purchased by visiting our website at store.astd.org or by calling 800.628.2783 or 703.683.8100.

Library of Congress Control Number: 2007937426

ISBN-10: 1-56286-463-7
ISBN-13: 978-1-56286-463-7

ASTD Press Editorial Staff
Director: Cat Russo
Manager, Acquisitions & Author Relations: Mark Morrow
Editorial Manager: Jacqueline Edlund-Braun
Editorial Assistant: Kelly Norris
Copyeditor: Christine Cotting
Indexer: April Davis
Proofreader: Kris Patenaude
Interior Design and Production: UpperCase Publication Services, Ltd.
Pig Tales Illustrator: Corey Wilkinson, Wilkinson Brothers Inc., Hardworking Design
Cover Design: Renita Wade

CONTENTS

10 STEPS TO SUCCESS

Let's face it, most people spend their days in chaotic, fast-paced, time- and resource-strained organizations. Finding time for just one more project, assignment, or even learning opportunity—no matter how career enhancing or useful—is difficult to imagine. The *10 Steps* series is designed for today's busy professional who needs advice and guidance on a wide array of topics ranging from project management to people management, from business planning strategy to decision making and time management, from return-on-investment to conducting organizational surveys and questionnaires. Each book in this ASTD series promises to take its readers on a journey to basic understanding, with practical application the ultimate destination. This is truly a just-tell-me-what-to-do-now series. You will find action-driven language teamed with examples, worksheets, case studies, and tools to help you quickly implement the right steps and chart a path to your own success. The *10 Steps* series will appeal to a broad business audience from middle managers to upper-level management. Workplace learning and human resource professionals along with other professionals seeking to improve their value proposition in their organizations will find these books a great resource.

P R E F A C E

Like yours, my business life and my personal life have been very chaotic this year. Ironically, I have been writing this project management book, offering others advice about how to juggle all the projects in their lives while I haven't been doing a very good juggling job myself. I love teaching project management, and this, my third book on the topic, has enabled me to do what I love and has helped me get my own project management back where it should be. I hope it will be helpful to you in the same way.

I work in the real world. Academic project management is a nice starting place, but not enough for the complexity of the things that I want to manage. As I speak, the dog is scratching the door and my husband is rewiring the stereo system at full volume in the family room. My teenager's boyfriend will be here any minute and then we're all off to church later this evening. One daughter wants me to look at the IKEA website and help her (with my credit card) redesign her room. The other daughter wants me to help her load CDs on her new Chocolate cell phone. It's the week after Christmas, and the decorations are piled in the hall, near a foothill of laundry. Been here?

Professionally, my 20-year-old consulting company, Russell Martin & Associates, has been redefined at least 20 times. Right now, project management is critical to our ability to survive and grow. Like you, I didn't have time to do anything else, especially write a book. Sales were slow last year and we were scrambling to evolve our marketing strategy and product focus. Around this time, I heard David Norton speak. He shared this statistic: less than 10 percent of all companies successfully implement their strategies. I was convinced that if we could not implement our strategy, we'd be closed by the end of 2006. It was also motivating to hear that most of our competitors were likely to be unsuccessful at their strategies.

I organized our strategy into projects and explicitly named project and task managers. My staff are not project managers, and I had overestimated how much they understood (ironic, since we are so busy teaching others!). We prioritized our projects and worked the plan. Making the transition to this approach is still evolving; unfortunately, you can't just create a plan and then walk away. The edges are always shifting. We often revisit the questions, What is a project? and Where does everything else go? But we've made dramatic changes, and I'm more confident that people move through change more easily when it's clear what is expected of them. This directive clarity is what project management brings.

The point is to *communicate*. The more chaos, the more temptation to run and hide, but the more critical it is to communicate. In my business this has been a constant challenge. In our customers' businesses, it's exponentially more challenging.

Complex project management software, techniques, and methods are very useful when you're doing large, "cross-silo," mission-critical projects. We've worked with very large, global customers who have tried to implement rigorous, cross-functional project management strategies. They attempt to go from anarchy (everyone doing what they want) to dictatorship (everyone blindly following the process), but eventually find they need to come back to the middle—to real project management. That's my expertise.

In a sense, my company has carved a niche translating academic/theoretical project management to real-life project managers in the business trenches. We provide project management learning to training organizations, information technology (IT) units, and often entire corporations. A good project manager cannot hide behind a methodology. Good project management requires a person who can think, a person who knows how to pick the best approach for a specific project. You'll find in this book that my 10 steps parallel a rigorous approach while backing off the complexity a bit.

These same large project management tools and techniques can be roadblocks when you're managing the kinds of projects filling most of your personal project portfolio. I've tried to write a book to share with you a "slimmed-down" version of the best of project management. I know that if you implement any one of these steps, your project success will improve; and if you implement all of them, you'll be much more successful than you are now.

Many of you are unexpected project managers. Although you never dreamed you'd be a project manager, suddenly your whole work life revolves around projects. You're the manager on some of these projects, some you participate in, and you compete with others for scant resources. The project manager with the organizational skills necessary to manage this project maze will thrive. That's what I hope this book will help you develop—the ability to navigate the real world of your projects.

This book and companion CD-ROM are my attempt to outline the 10 most important things that a person needs to do to improve his or her capacity and reduce the stress level. Whether it's your workload or your family schedule, it's not likely that the amount of chaos is going to diminish soon. What I've written here is not an organizational approach, but it will fit nicely into whatever policy your company has. Most of our customers feel the same way. Most have implemented a formal project management methodology but have not been able to realize the hoped-for benefits.

And now it's your turn, reader. Use this book to become more resilient and agile. Practice flexible structure—at all times have a plan for focus, but always be ready to change when the situation dictates. Learn to sit quietly and think rather than just jump up and do. Feel free to contact me with your questions as you learn. (My email address is lou@russellmartin.com, and my phone number is 317.475.9311.) I'll be working on these things with you. Peace.

Acknowledgments

My ability to manage projects is only as good as my home team. Thanks to Doug, Kelly, Kristin, and Katherine for keeping it all together as I sneaked out to write early every morning. I am most proud of my family project.

Thanks, also, to Mark Morrow (my editor at ASTD) for patience as I worked through this book and my challenges this year. Mark, you are a good friend.

Thanks to Margie Brown, Vija Dixon, Carol Mason, and our newest team member Tina Osborn for undying support and energy in making our transition from an event-oriented to a project-oriented company.

This year, I've had the privilege to employ and work with some unbelievably good project managers. I would like to thank Mary Cook, Janice Daly, and Susan Vaughn for sharing their abilities to manage complexity and change.

Huge thanks to Christine Cotting, editor-extraordinaire, able to make you laugh while you're avoiding your writing. She has become a dear friend through this adventure.

Finally, I dedicate this book to the other side of my brain, Vija Dixon, who is beginning the most courageous fight of her life. PHAO (Pray Hard and Often).

Lou Russell
May 2007

I N T R O D U C T O N

When you improve your capacity to manage projects, you affect a large chunk of your life, so my goal for you as you move through this book has two parts:

1. that you realize how much of your time actually is spent on project management, both at work and at home
2. that you learn simple, useful ways to improve your project management velocity.

When you go looking for a book on project management, you have a lot of choices, but many of the books are written for people who are certified project managers or are running large organizationwide projects at global companies. Many of us need a complementary but simpler approach.

I've found expert information in surprising places, from NASA to the women who run the Christmas drive at church. One of the metaphors from NASA that influenced my thinking a great deal is the story of the Three Little Pigs.

Discovering the Basic Principles of Project Management

NASA has a wonderful web magazine called *ASK* that it uses to share lessons learned on projects. At the January 2006 Professional Development Conference of the National Society of Professional Engineers, NASA's administrator Michael D. Griffin described *ASK* in this way:

One of the innovations of the Academy is the Academy Sharing Knowledge, or *ASK* magazine, which gives NASA managers the opportunity to swiftly tell each other about successes, failures and lessons learned. These "after action reports" were featured in a recent issue of *Government Executive Magazine* as a model for what every federal manager should be able to tap into. (http://www.nasa.gov/pdf/141294main_NSPE_19_Jan_06.pdf)

This award-winning magazine is available to all of us at http://ap pel.nasa.gov/ask/.

A few years ago, Dr. Edward Hoffman edited an early version of the magazine, and he challenged my project management thought process with an editorial about the Three Little Pigs and project management. Here is an excerpt of that editorial:

> Remember the fairy tale, "The Three Little Pigs," and how the first pig built a house of straw? Nice, light, cost-conscious straw. The only problem was the hungry wolf that came along one day and knocked on the door. The wolf asked to be let in, and the pig quite reasonably replied, "Not by the hair of my chinny, chin, chin." Unfortunately, the wolf simply huffed and puffed and blew the straw house down, and pig number one had to shake his bacon to get to the second pig's house.
>
> The second pig had nominally improved the quality of construction by using wood. Once again, however, the pigs were forced to scurry when the wolf's resolve proved stronger than the structure. In the end, our pigs were saved by the foresight, concern for quality and use of top materials by the third pig, who had built his house of brick. The wolf could not get into the house and the pigs survived, presumably to live happily ever after.
>
> At first glance, the lessons are obvious. Be industrious, plan for future threats and never short-change quality specifications. On further review, the difficulty and risks

of project planning are much more complex. (http://
appel.nasa.gov/ask/issues/11/overview/ask11_resources_
di rectorsdesk.html)

Since childhood we have heard this story and been clearly
taught that the two pigs who were lazy and cheap were wrong. The
hero of the tale was the pig who took the time to plan and deliver
a top-quality brick house. The admonition given to us as children
through this story has influenced our project management beliefs
as adults: We expect organizations managing projects to approach
their work with the same methodical and ultimately successful set
of steps that the wise pig used, and we expect these steps to emu-
late NASA's legendary success. After all, it was NASA that put men
on the moon using less computing power than most high-end calcu-
lators have today. Still, however, we all have a nagging voice in our
minds telling us that our business will not allow this expensive focus on quality.

NASA itself has had similar challenges recently. NASA has en-
joyed a number of project successes since their Apollo achievements,
but it also has suffered some tragic setbacks, such as the shuttle dis-
asters. The reasons for project failures at NASA are complex and include faulty oversight, arrogance, and budget cuts—or, more accurately, the real world of project planning. Many of these specific
challenges are discussed with surprising candor in *ASK* magazine.

Hoffman challenges us to look deeper at the players. The "quality" pig would not have been the star had it not been for the wolf.

Imagine the story without the wolf. Suddenly, the third
pig becomes a goat. His mug appears on the cover of
newspapers exposing and criticizing the flagrant and ex-
cessive costs of the brick house. Pigs one and two are
lauded for exceptional and efficient construction management, while pig three is used as a case study in mis-
management. The wolf is so vital to the definition of
success that one might be led to wonder if pig three contracted with the wolf to harass and threaten the others.

The wolf represents the constraints of this construction project. Like a well-run business, the wise wolf builds a project that meets the unique need at that point in time—in this story, a wolf with very strong breath.

Each of us struggles with our own constraints on our own projects. Many novice project managers try to ignore them, hoping they'll just go away. They don't. Constraints require us to be flexible in implementing a project management structure that will move us through chaos to success. And our encounters with those constraints teach us that there is no single path to project management success. Each project is unique. Each project comes with different wolves.

The constraints come from the business. The project may have to be done quickly to meet a regulatory requirement. The project may need to be done on a limited budget because the competitive market demands a cheaper product. The project may have to be done at high quality because people's lives are at stake. Each project has its own constraints dictated by strategy and the marketplace.

Because the constraints are dictated by the business, successful project management comes from a collaboration nurtured by ongoing communication with the business. In today's frantic business environment, there's nothing more challenging than communication. To address that challenge, this book will help you set the stage early for collaboration with your sponsors, and help you continue communicating through the unpredictable surprises that arise. And here's something that adds to the overall complexity: it isn't all that rare for a constraint to change after a project has started!

The business tells the project manager the reason that money is being allotted and spent on this project instead of on something else. Initiating this conversation and understanding the business case reveal both the business constraints and the expected business impact of project success. This gives the project manager the background to make adjustments when the project runs into bumps along the way.

You will learn how to build a plan based on your project's specific business need. Because all projects are unique, each project plan will be different from any other project plan you have built. The model for project management that you'll learn from this book will be the same, but the way you apply it will depend on the specific business opportunity you're addressing.

You'll learn that, after the project begins, everything will change. Your ability to practice '"flexible structure" will be tested. Finally, you'll learn how to end a project, and how to review lessons gained from the experience.

This book is full of checklists, diagramming techniques, models, and processes to help you through each phase of the project. You'll discover, however, that project management is all about relationships and communication, and that using tools, techniques, and processes alone won't guarantee success. A fool with a great technique is still a fool. Projects succeed or fail because of *people*.

And you'll learn to expect the unexpected. Project management is about risk mitigation, and you have to identify and react to project risk in ways that build rather than destroy collaboration. Again in the words of Hoffman:

> In any event, the uncertainty of future events makes project planning a slippery endeavor. Was the third pig a better strategic and tactical planner, or just lucky? Did the use of risk management techniques indicate the probability of marauding wolves? Was the selection of brick based on a cost-benefit analysis of the situation? One will never know. That sort of background information wasn't included in the fairy tale.
>
> One thing we can say for certain is that experienced project managers realize that environmental realities figure prominently when determining what risks jeopardize a project. To what extent they plan for a wolf at the door probably depends on what experience they have that a wolf will show up there. The dilemma all project managers face is deciding which risks are too costly to

It will be best to read
Steps 1 through 10
in order so you are
clear how the pieces
fit together. Resist
the initial urge to
skip around.

plan for and which ones are too costly
not to plan for.

What You'll Find in This Book

I've broken the project management process
into 10 steps and covered each step separately. You'll get the most out of the book if
you first read it through without skipping
around. I also recommend that you select a current project on
which to work the steps for practice. When you've read the book
from beginning to end, you'll be able to jump around to the steps
you need when you need them. Use table I.1 to figure out where to
go to review material for specific issues.

An Overview of the 10 Steps

Here is a brief overview of the 10 steps to successful project management:

◆ **Step 1: Decide If You Have a Real Project to Manage—**
Many of the students in my classes are there because
they've unexpectedly become project managers. They never
planned for this role, but now find that they spend most of
their time working on projects. Here you'll learn how to tell
the difference between a task, a process, and a project.
Many of the things now on your to-do list really aren't
tasks—they're projects. By treating them as such, you'll
work more effectively.

◆ **Step 2: Prove Your Project Is Worth Your Time—**In both
profit and nonprofit entities, there is a limited amount of
money and a finite number of people to get things done.
Here you'll learn how to discern and document the business
reason for the project. When you understand the financial
part of project management, you clearly will see the impact
of projects that wrap up late or come in over budget.

TABLE I.1

Issues Addressed by Specific Steps

Issue	Step	General Advice
You want to learn how to start a project well	2, 3, 4	Investing energy and effort at the beginning of a project pays off at the end.
You want to learn how to plan a project well	5, 6	It helps to build a project plan based on the business constraints.
You want to learn how to manage a project that is under way	7, 8	Practice *flexible structure:* at all times, have a plan but be ready to bend it when project conditions dictate.
You want to learn how to end a project	9	Communicate clearly when a project is done.
You want to grow your own project management competency	10	Conducting a post-project review will jump-start your competency—even if you do the review alone.
You're overwhelmed with work and don't feel that you're making any progress	1	You may be managing *tasks* rather than projects. Organizing and prioritizing your work by project will improve your ability to deliver more work.
You've been assigned a project, but have not been told why this project suddenly is funded	2	Most project managers are not very aware of the financial impact of their projects. It's important that the company clearly defines the anticipated return-on-investment for each project; it's equally important that the project manager be aware of this expectation.
You feel that the project boundaries are shifting continually, and that the size of the project is in-creasing without an equal increase in time and budget	3	The primary killer of project success is *scope creep.* Even if it's late in the project, it's never too late to stop and define the scope with the stakeholders. Negotiating more time and money requires a joint

continued on next page

Table I.1, continued

Issue	Step	General Advice
		agreement on the scope of the project.
A nervous little voice in your head is asking if this project can be done successfully	4	Your little voice is always right. It's critical that you take time to brainstorm possible risks that may challenge project success because it gives you the opportunity to build a mitigation plan to avoid or react to those risks. You won't guess all of them, but you'll be ready for most.
Members of the project team spend all their time fighting among themselves or avoiding each other	5	Companies are organized to compete across functional areas for resources. These dynamics can paralyze a project, so the project manager must nurture collaboration—it's the only way to success.
It's difficult to coordinate the array of things that different people are doing on this project, and sometimes a late activity slows down someone else	6	Creating a project plan informs everyone on the project about exactly what's expected of them, when it's due, and how it affects others. Without a solid plan, individuals either will get distracted by other work or will repeatedly interrupt the project manager for information or direction.
You just got a major change to the project requirements, and you're afraid you won't complete the project on time	7	Project managers must learn to think in contingency terms. Contingency planning is an in-the-moment type of risk management. When change occurs in a project, the project manager must have two or three alternatives to keep the project on track.
The stakeholders keep changing their minds about what they want, and the project is stalled by all the chaos	8	Chaos is the norm in project management, not the exception. Businesses must react at the speed of the Internet to market trends, and this makes the requirements of many projects

Table I.1, continued

Issue	Step	General Advice
		unstable at best. Flexible structure is an important key to accepting chaos and managing through it.
You finished your project a month ago, but the stakeholders keep coming in with small changes.	9	It seems like a simple concept, but "done" is a tough thing to define for projects. Learn to establish a project's completion criteria and to communicate and reinforce them effectively.
It seems as if the same mistakes are repeated on every project	10	Learning how best to invest the time in a post-project review will increase your project manage-ment competency and that of the business.

◆ **Step 3: Manage Scope Creep**—Ask 100 people if docu-menting scope is critical to project success and I bet that 99 percent of them would say "yes." I also think that at least 70 percent don't document scope at all. Most people feel that describing the scope in writing requires difficult conversations with busy executives and page after page of contract-like text demanding sign-off. They assume it's bet-ter just to get going on the project. They're wrong. Here you'll discover how to document scope graphically to en-hance communication and limit scope creep.

◆ **Step 4: Identify, Rate, and Manage Risks**—A project risk is something that could happen during the project, and it's something you make plans to mitigate or avoid. By brain-storming at the outset about what could go wrong during the project and how such situations might be managed or mitigated, you take some of the pain of interruption out of project work. Remember, however, that you'll never think of everything that might happen on a project, and sometimes it's not worth the extra energy to preplan for a risk that is not very likely or won't have a great impact. Here you'll learn how to brainstorm and to prioritize risk mitigation.

♦ **Step 5: Collaborate Successfully**—One of the most important things I've learned about project management is the usefulness of collaboration. It sounds simple but, in practice, collaboration is extremely difficult. There will be many times when you're angry with someone on the team or with one of the stakeholders because a promise has been broken, a change has been made, or some other bomb has been dropped. At this moment of anger, you choose between collaboration and payback (a project killer). Here you'll find how to take a deep breath and create collaboration without regard to the turmoil and personal agendas.

♦ **Step 6: Gather Your Team and Make a Schedule**—In many project management classes, you learn how to make a work breakdown structure to brainstorm the tasks needed in a project, and then how to hook all the tasks together along a timeline. It's a good academic exercise but is rarely done in the real world. On an actual project, you're given the end date and a bank of resources that usually seem unreasonable and inadequate, respectively, and you have to fit the tasks you want to do into that tight space. In this step you'll learn how to create a plan from a fixed date, a fixed budget, and constrained resources.

♦ **Step 7: Adjust Your Schedule**—When the project starts, it's challenging to monitor how it's going. Project status meetings can become "who hunts" in which participants spend the entire meeting figuring out who's at fault. Keeping track of all the people whose work you need at critical times is very difficult. Here you'll learn quick, repeatable ways to communicate status and keep everyone aligned with the project. You'll discover some warning signs that reveal the project is drifting into trouble. And we'll take a look at the importance of conducting those difficult conversations that can get your project back on track.

♦ **Step 8: Embrace the Natural Chaos of People**—Chaos happens—that's a given. But chaos really is just the result of people changing their minds, getting angry and frustrated, misunderstanding directions, and working under stress. Here you'll learn the people skills required to build relationships, manage conflict, and negotiate disagreements.

◆ **Step 9: Know When You're Done**—Ending a project doesn't begin when the project is complete; it begins in Steps 1 through 4. Clearly defining and communicating what "done" means throughout a project are critical aspects of ending well. This step helps you define and communicate clear completion criteria.

◆ **Step 10: Follow Up to Learn Lessons**—The most important and least practiced project management skill is the ability to do a post-project review. Having the discipline to set aside time and reflect on a project, alone or with others, ensures that future projects will be better managed. In this step you'll learn to apply a standard template to help capture lessons learned during the project. You'll also learn when and how to facilitate a follow-up discussion.

Topics Covered in the Steps

You'll find the following topics covered in most of the steps:

◆ *Time to Complete*—gives the project manager a general sense of how long it will take to finish the work in a step and describes the factors that influence the time required.

◆ *Stakeholders*—describes those who have a vested interest in the project. This section helps you identify the people with whom you should spend most of your limited time, especially those with whom you'll need to communicate most frequently.

◆ *Questions to Ask*—tells you what to ask and of whom to ask it. This section helps you pose well-thought-out questions about the project requirements. Succinct and appropriate questions show your respect for your stakeholders by taking as little of their time as possible.

◆ *Project Manager's Toolkit*—presents the tools, techniques, and processes you'll use to accomplish the step successfully.

You can try out everything you find in this section on your own current project.

◆ *Communication*—explains how and what to communicate in the step. In earlier sections, you've read about stakeholders, the questions to ask them, and the tools and techniques you'll use to complete the step. Communication includes determining what questions or documents will be sent to stakeholders either to get their feedback or to keep them in the loop about the project's status.

◆ *What If I Skip This Step?*—describes the risk you take if you skip a specific step in managing the project. This section helps you make a conscious evaluation of potential shortcuts, realizing that there may be times when it makes sense to skip some steps.

◆ *Lurking Landmines*—points out common problems that may occur in the step. This section shows you that "surprises" are predictable.

◆ *Step Checklist*—offers a quick review of the step. Use this as you grow in project management competency to make sure that you haven't forgotten critical activities in the step.

Finally, you will find many other elements, including pointers, tools, tables, figures, worksheets, and examples that show you how to use tools and techniques. These valuable resources are provided for you to print out from the companion CD-ROM. To provide you with a practical sample, I'll use a blog project as the case study throughout the steps.

The Dare Model of Project Management

In this book you'll read about my project management model. It's called the Dare to Properly Manage Resources Model—the Dare Model, for short (*Project Management for Trainers*, ASTD, 2000). The model has these four phases:

1. **Define**—Explain why the business is committing resources to this project instead of spending the money on something else.

2. **Plan**—Given the business need, describe how people and other resources will be assigned to project tasks.

3. **Manage**—Adapt to the changing project by practicing "flexible structure." This is a phrase I use to explain a dichotomy in managing projects: At all times you have a plan (structure), but at all times you're ready to adapt the plan (flexible) when it no longer meets the needs of the business. You'll find this phrase often in the descriptions of tools and techniques that build adaptability into the project management process.

4. **Review**—Learn from the project experiences to grow future project success.

You'll find a schematic of this model in Step 1 (figure 1.2), with lists of tasks for each phase. This model is based on the Project Management Body of Knowledge (PMBOK) published and supported by the Project Management Institute (www.pmi.org). The 10 steps in this book are consistent with the PMBOK as well. You'll read a more complete explanation of this model in Step 1.

The Three Pigs

You'll find in each of the steps that I adapt the tale of the Three Little Pigs to illustrate some common project dynamics. I've also used the story in a few places to give you practice in one or another aspect of project management. You won't miss any crucial information if you skip the stories, but you may find it comforting to know that you're not the first person to see insanity on a project. I've named the three pigs to illustrate their focus and their project management style: *Speedy* likes to do things fast, *Goldy* likes to save money, and *Demmy* (with homage to W. Edwards Deming) likes high-quality work. As their adventures with BB Wolf unfold, you'll read how each of these types of project managers adds value and makes mistakes on every project.

One Caveat Before You Begin

If you were hoping for an infallible and reproducible to-do list that guarantees your success on any project with any constraints, you won't find it here. Some projects are impossible. I've never been on one, but I have had customers who have. In most cases, there are alternatives and creative adjustments that can make an impossible project possible. And many projects, although possible, are very difficult.

Every project is unique, and every one will present you with something you've never had to deal with before. I once heard information technology consultant Tim Lister say, "If you do two different projects the same way, you have done both incorrectly." My experience confirms that. I do apply the same model to all my projects, but the detail work in each one is completely different because the people and business issues involved are unique.

A good project management approach, combined with appropriately used tools and techniques chosen by a good project manager, creates project management success. To that end, I make the following assumptions in offering you this book:
- You really want to be successful with your projects.
- You're willing to step up and be accountable for that success.
- You're willing to learn and grow as a project manager.
- You're willing to become more agile and collaborative in that journey.

If this sounds like you, I'm excited to share with you my successes and failures in project management. Our guiding principle going forward will be *flexible structure*. At all times, we'll have a plan for making a project successful, and at all times, we'll be willing to adapt that plan and create a new plan when everything changes.

Decide If You Have a Real Project to Manage

In the mid-1990s, companies were beginning to create e-commerce sites. As the owner of a small business, I felt that we would need an e-commerce site as well. Whenever I have an idea of something I'd like to do, I throw it in my task list to make sure I don't forget it. I always put a reminder date on it, so that it pops up in a couple of weeks when I'll (supposedly) have more time to deal with it. "Build e-commerce site" continued to pop up every two weeks for a couple of months. My response was to add a couple of weeks to the date and push it out again.

Think about what putting something on your task list means. When I added that item, I thought that someday I'd find myself with an hour of uninterrupted time and I'd just knock out an e-commerce site. In those terms, that's ridiculous. Building such a website was pretty time consuming and complex, and it certainly couldn't be checked off in an hour or so. The real reason that task resisted completion was that I never took the time to break it into the steps necessary to complete it.

Happy Dale Pig Farm

was a very safe place. Ma and Pa Oink nestled their brood of three beautiful piglets together in a corner of the barnyard. Even as babies, the piglets showed very different personalities. First-born Speedy was always on the move, getting himself into everything. Goldy, the middle child, hoarded little found items in piles away from the others. Demmy, the youngest, was practical and very organized. He helped his pig-sibs and the other babies in the yard when they got into trouble. Even the plucky little chicks depended on Demmy to teach them the ways of the farm.

But over one seemingly cozy night, everything at Happy Dale changed. New managers took over the farm—folks who drove sleek black sedans instead of pickup trucks and wore Armani instead of overalls. The pigs were shoved into tiny pens in long, metal barns. They weren't allowed outside and spent their days eating and sleeping. Rumor had it that even the chickens were in prison.

The Oinks were worried, but they thought it best that the family stick together and wait for these new people to move on and for Happy Dale life to return to normal. At least inside they were protected from that infamous BB Wolf. They'd heard the chickens' stories about relatives who'd wandered too close to the fences, and the Oinks knew BB would eat them all up if they left the farm.

For his part, Demmy didn't see it the way his parents did. He thought the farm managers seemed content with the "new normal," and he didn't believe things would ever return to the way they'd been before. Demmy was a little pig with a big dream of a better life, and he was willing to trade safety for satisfaction. He'd risk a run-in with BB Wolf. He figured a good plan would help him avoid the wolf and recover the freedom he remembered.

So, while the older Oinks snuffled and shifted in their sleep the next moonless night, Demmy woke his brothers, whispered his plan, and wiggled with Speedy and Goldy through the door slats and out of the not-so-happy dale.

In his classic book, *The 7 Habits of Highly Effective People,* Stephen Covey (2004) illustrated the difference between strategic (important and non-urgent) and tactical (important and urgent) activities (figure 1.1). He explained that the more discipline we have to complete strategic activities, the less firefighting we do, thereby reducing the number of tactical activities that interrupt us daily. Many of the important activities lurking on your to-do list actually are strategic projects. As the tactical, easily checked-off tasks monopolize our time, we get more and more behind.

As I write this, I'm reminded of a task on my list that I've pushed off continually for a couple of years now: join a few speakers' bureaus. I have delegated some of the first steps but never have taken the time to really manage this as a project. This is the year!

Projects vs. Tasks

In today's chaotic business climate, multitasking is the norm. Jobs have been trimmed and companies are doing more with less. The roles and responsibilities have to evolve to deal with the chaos; they cannot be defined clearly enough before there is a need to adapt again. People are juggling multiple projects and often acting as both project manager and team. More frequently, people are

FIGURE 1.1

Strategic and Tactical Tasks

Important / Urgent Tasks	Important / Non-urgent Tasks
Tactical Emergencies	*Strategic Initiatives*
Not Important / Urgent Tasks	**Not Important / Non-urgent Tasks**
Other People's Fires—Don't Do	*Time Wasters—Don't Do*

Source: Based on Stephen R. Covey, *The 7 Habits of Highly Effective People* (New York: Free Press, 2004).

feeling completely overwhelmed by the amount of work always waiting for them.

David Allen, a noted author and consultant, does a great job in his articles and books describing the difference between a *task* and a *project*. He says, "Most people are inefficient because they don't force themselves to decide what things mean and what they are actually going to do about them when they first show up. So they are constantly rethinking the same things over and over and not making any progress in doing so—only adding to their stress" (http://www.davidco.com/faq.php?detail=32&category=5#question32).

In truth, most people are responsible for more projects than they are even aware of. Think of some of the tasks that are currently on your to-do list. Chances are, if there is an undone item that has been on the list for a while, it's really a project, not a task. Worksheet 1.1 offers a set of questions to help you decide if an activity is a task or a project.

Treating a project as a task prevents you from clearly defining the multiple steps and time commitment necessary to complete it. That creates the following problems:

- You avoid the task because you really haven't figured out how to do it.
- You do small bits of the task but never get the momentum to see it all the way through.
- Your to-do list stays jammed with stuff you never get to, adding to your stress and making your list almost impossible to use.
- Every new task you get adds to your feeling that you've lost control.

Many people are struggling to balance a task list that's really a project list. Take a minute and see if you can tell the difference. Which of these are projects and which are tasks?

- making cookies
- writing a status report
- coding a webpage
- drawing a blueprint
- cooking Thanksgiving dinner
- preparing a status meeting
- creating a website
- developing a new product.

WORKSHEET 1.1

Is It a Task or a Project?

Instructions: Answer the following questions for each activity. Then consult the scoring section to learn if your activity is a task or a project.

1. Can you complete the activity in one sitting?   Yes ☐   No ☐

2. Can you do the activity without anyone else's help?   Yes ☐   No ☐

3. Can you complete the activity in less than four hours?   Yes ☐   No ☐

4. Has the activity been on your to-do list for less than a month?   Yes ☐   No ☐

5. Can you clearly define the measurements you will use to determine that the task is done?   Yes ☐   No ☐

Scoring

* If you answered "yes" to the majority of the questions, your activity is a task.

* If you answered "no" to three or more of the questions, treat your activity like a project. Follow Steps 1 through 10 to get it done.

Clearly, the tasks are on the left and the projects are on the right. But there also are many things we do that sit squarely in between —and that's where we often lose our way.

What Is a Project?

The Project Management Body of Knowledge (PMBOK) is an internationally recognized standard setting forth the fundamental processes and best practices of project management. It describes a project in this way:

> A project is a temporary endeavor undertaken to achieve a particular aim and to which project management can be applied, regardless of the project's size, budget, or timeline. (www.pmi.org)

Let's look more closely at the critical points in that definition:

- *temporary endeavor:* a project does not go on forever
- *achieve a particular aim:* a project must have a goal for completion
- *size, budget, timeline:* a project demands that you manage the need that's driving the project—money, people, and deadlines.

Here are the critical differences between a project and other work that you do:

- A project has a definable beginning and a definable end.
- A project has cost, time, and quality goals for completion.
- A project requires the use of part-time resources that you may or may not have direct authority to use.

People often confuse a *project* and a *process*. The key difference between them is this: a project begins and ends; a process continues without a definable conclusion. Both comprise tasks, but the tasks of a process are repeatable—in other words, you follow roughly the same tasks every time you do the process. For example, when a project team develops a new suite of software to track customer contacts, they are working on a project—it starts and then ends when the software is installed. When the sales staff uses that software to manage its client base, they are using a process.

At the start of this step, you read about differentiating between a task and a project. Now let's see if you grasp the differences between a project and a process. Put a checkmark beside the activities that are *not* projects:

- ☐ 1. Creating processes to ensure business compliance
- ☐ 2. Following processes to ensure business compliance
- ☐ 3. Planning and holding a company sales retreat
- ☐ 4. Following the project management standards
- ☐ 5. Devising a new training course
- ☐ 6. Teaching a new training course

Activities 2, 4, and 6 are not projects because they don't end—you do them over and over again. They're processes used to deal with things in a routine way—it's ongoing work.

When a new project is started, you follow a project management process to see that all the steps needed to complete the project successfully happen, including tasks to plan, organize, and control. In Step 5 you'll learn how to identify the various activities that a project requires.

Each project is unique. Each project has a set of tasks necessary to complete it successfully. Some of these tasks will be things that you do for all projects, including the 10 steps in this book. Some of these tasks will be specific to one project you're managing. For example, a project to design a new website will include many tasks that aren't included in a project to build an office building. A project intended to be done quickly will take shortcuts that a project intended to produce a high-quality end product will not. The basic 10 steps of this book, however, will be applicable to *all* of your projects.

Benefits of Project Management

A defined process for managing a project, like the 10 steps described in this book, increases
- repeatability of project success
- scalability of project work
- ability to manage complexity
- ability to react agilely to business change
- your clear focus on business results.

The trick is to follow a process that gives you enough structure to jump-start your project plan without adding too much overhead and expense. Companies new to the project perspective usually start with everyone doing his or her own thing with his or her project (also known as anarchy). Eventually, that approach breaks under the cost of redundant work across disconnected projects that can't communicate with each other.

As their projects get more stressful, novice project managers often waste time by
- filling out forms they don't understand
- hiding from or ignoring the customer's perspective

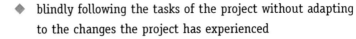

- blindly following the tasks of the project without adapting to the changes the project has experienced
- delivering late, poor-quality, or over-budget work.

Next, companies usually overcorrect with a strict, document-intense approach to project management. They add such extensive structure that project teams find themselves doing the project management deliverables and never getting to the actual project work. For example, if you spend all your time documenting the scope of the project, the risk mitigation plan, and the communications plan but never actually start building anything, you're not focusing on the right things. When a project management approach is too complex, people lose track of the difference between doing project management to help streamline a successful project and doing project management because the boss said so.

The best place to be is in the middle of these two extremes—a comfortable and productive middle ground between hands-off and hands-tied. When done correctly, project management encourages more thinking up front to ensure more success at implementation. Nothing is done by a good project manager just because it's "supposed to be." Every step in a good project management approach has a clear purpose. This kind of approach encourages

- less rework
- better quality
- less cost to the business
- less chaos
- fewer heroics.

A good project management process, with flexibility *and* structure, ensures that your project will

- increase the bottom line by keeping the decision-making focus on the customer and building customer loyalty through project completion that is on time and within budget
- avoid costs by estimating rework through consistent management of deliverables and streamlining project success through lessons learned and evolving processes

* improve service by rapidly escalating and resolving issues and driving cross-organizational accountability.

Roles of Project Management

Think about actors in a drama. Playing a role means inhabiting a part. There are specific behaviors, characteristics, and boundaries for each role. Likewise, in a project, there are specific roles to be taken and it's important that everyone knows what she or he is responsible for producing or overseeing. Depending on the size and complexity of the project, one person may play one or several roles. In very large projects, one role may be played by several people. The only exception is the role of project manager. Research clearly shows that there should be *only one* project manager.

At this point, you've started to think about those tasks on your to-do list that probably are projects. Now you're an unintended project manager with a list of projects rather than a task list, so what does that change? One of the most important changes is how you view yourself. Thinking of yourself as a manager of projects is different from thinking of yourself as a manager of tasks. In reality, you probably juggle both roles daily.

What does a *project manager* do? His or her primary responsibilities are to plan, organize, and control a project to its successful completion. To do this, the project manager

* figures out what work needs to be done
* finds and allocates the right resources to the right work
* manages the communication among all the people involved
* adjusts the plan when the project requirements change.

The project manager's role includes managing the team. This requires leadership skills, including setting the team vision, assigning the best people to the tasks, coaching, and resolving conflict.

Although the role of project manager is a critical one, it sometimes can be misinterpreted as the most important role. The project manager may forget that he or she doesn't own the project. The business, represented by an executive funding the work, is the project's owner. The project manager is the *steward* of the project, essentially watching and guiding it.

Chances are you have become a project manager because you've been successful at the work you do. Many organizations promote to project managers those people who have shown great success getting tasks done. It's most likely that some of the projects you manage will require you to act as project manager *and* the entire project team. When this happens, you'll be tempted to neglect the strategic aspect of the project manager's role and immerse yourself in the "doing" role of the project team. Resist that urge because both roles are vital to the success of any project. In Step 4 you'll learn how much time to spend on project management activities by identifying and using the risk of a project to anticipate the amount of time demanded.

> Many companies use the terms *project leader* and *project manager* interchangeably. The PMBOK uses them to imply hierarchy, with the project manager responsible for the entire project, and project leaders responsible for specific subsections of the project.

I like to describe this in a way that's more relevant to my life: The project manager is the nanny, and the project (aka, the kids) belongs to the business (the parents). This differentiation matters because there is a big difference between the decisions a nanny makes regarding the children and the decisions that parents make for their children. In just the same way, important decisions about the business benefit of a project always should be made by the business, not the project manager. There will be more discussion on this later in the book, but you should know that it's very common for the project manager to feel pressure to make these decisions without the necessary information.

The person (or people) who represents the business and writes the checks for the project is called the *project sponsor*. She or he
◆ establishes the business case
◆ approves project adjustments

◆ works with the project manager to resolve conflicts between parts of the business.

The project sponsor has requested the work so he clearly can define the business case for the investment. You may have a project on your list that you're funding yourself, but in most cases the project sponsor is a senior leader in your organization. It's possible to play the role of project sponsor and project manager, but that happens mostly in smaller organizations.

The sponsor owns the project—it's her vision, her request, and her money. As the manager, you'll handle the project, but it's not *your* project. This is a critical point. Many managers lose their way because they start to think that the project belongs to them. They make choices that should be made by the sponsor. They begin to avoid communication with the sponsor—in fact, they believe the sponsor is a barrier to their ability to do the project well. If any of that occurs, the project will struggle. It's very important for the manager to understand and accept the supporting nature of his or her role.

The project sponsor is an extremely important player, and if you don't know who it is, stop the project until you find out. At that point you may make the unhappy and disruptive discovery that no one has figured out who the sponsor is. Realistically, it may not be within your authority or ability to solve this problem, but it is certainly a serious risk factor that you must take to the people who can solve the problem—an effort we know in business as "escalating."

Sponsors tend to come from the executive ranks. The sponsor's rank in the organization ensures that he or she will be very busy and difficult to approach, but as project manager you need a strong relationship with the sponsor from the beginning. Many sponsors don't know what it means to be a sponsor so the manager has to help them understand the criticality of their role. Tool 1.1 shows tasks that the project manager can use to engage and keep the sponsor involved.

The other people who have vested interests in the project are called the *stakeholders*. These are people who, for one reason or

TOOL 1.1

Tasks for Engaging and Maintaining Sponsorship

* Review the project business benefit
* Review the project goals
* Ask for and schedule in advance regular meetings with the sponsor to ensure the project is on track, according to the current business priorities
* Create a list of expectations with the sponsor to clarify both roles
* Clarify how handoffs between the manager and sponsor will occur
* Clarify when and how project issues will be brought to the sponsor
* Clarify how you hope the sponsor will communicate the status of the project to peers and to the company leadership
* Determine how the project sponsor will judge the completion of the project
* Determine how the sponsor will participate in the post-project review.

another, care what happens to the project. They may supply some project resources or they may receive output from the project. For example, the billing staff in a doctor's office must be involved in rolling out HIPAA compliance. They may not be part of the project team designing the roll-out processes, but they have a vested interest.

By definition, the project sponsor is a stakeholder. So are the members of the project team and the manager. It's important to have a clear understanding of who the stakeholders are and to communicate with them regularly throughout the project.

You'll learn more about the project sponsor and stakeholders in Step 2, and you'll learn to clarify the project scope with them in Step 3. In addition, you'll learn how to determine the risk of the project based on the number of stakeholders and their priorities in Step 4—and that will help you build contingency plans before the project begins. In Step 8 you'll learn to negotiate and manage the conflict that naturally occurs among stakeholders during a project.

TOOL 1.2

Potential Project Team Roles

- Executive sponsor
- Project manager
- Project administrator
- Technical leader
- Quality assurance leader
- Business operations owner

- Business owner
- Architectural adviser
- Infrastructure adviser
- Finance leader
- Subject-matter expert

The *project team* comprises the people who are actively involved in the project tasks. Sometimes it's difficult to determine whether a person is external to the project team or part of it, and it's the project manager's responsibility to decide this by the amount of time the person spends on project activities. Tool 1.2 lists some of the roles that may exist on a project team.

Another key role on the project team is that of *project administrator*. In larger projects it's helpful to have a person who keeps track of all the project documentation, coordinates meetings, and monitors project task completion. This person reports to the project manager.

The heart of the project team is the group of individuals who do the work the project produces. They may be computer programmers, business analysts, training developers, or some other skilled practitioners. They too may forget that the part of the project they're working on ultimately belongs to the sponsor—an understanding that the project manager must carefully encourage.

POINTER

If you're both manager and project team, don't neglect the project manager role. Schedule a certain amount of time each week to think about the project and review your plan. If you don't do this, you may find that you've completed lots of tasks that add little value to what your project has changed into while you weren't watching.

In Step 5, you'll learn to build collaboration between the team members and the stakeholders. In Step 6, you'll assign project team members to tasks as you to build a project schedule.

The project manager's role includes managing the team. This requires leadership skills, including setting the team vision, assigning the best people to the tasks, coaching, and resolving conflict.

A Model for Project Management: Dare to Properly Manage Resources

Figure 1.2 shows the Dare to Properly Manage Resources Model that you first read about in the introduction to this book. The first letter of each word in the name—**DPMR**—will help you remember the four main phases of project management that will be discussed in the 10 steps. Those phases are *define, plan, manage,* and *review.*

By definition, a project has a beginning and end, as shown in the figure. In between those poles, four significant things should occur:

1. **Define:** This phase explores *why* the project is being done—that is, why is money being invested in this project instead of something else? What is the business case? The way in which the project is done (set out in the project plan) depends on why it is being done.
2. **Plan:** The planning phase establishes *how* the project will be done to meet the business goals defined in the first phase. The outcome of the planning activities, the project plan, specifies the tasks to be done and the people assigned to each task. Essentially it is the project schedule.
3. **Manage:** In this phase the project plan is carried out, and the word to remember is *adapt.* This is a little confusing, because a lot of work has to be done defining and planning before the project plan can start. During this phase, the project manager may find that the business case from the defining phase or the project plan from the planning

FIGURE 1.2

Schematic of the Dare to Properly Manage Resources Model

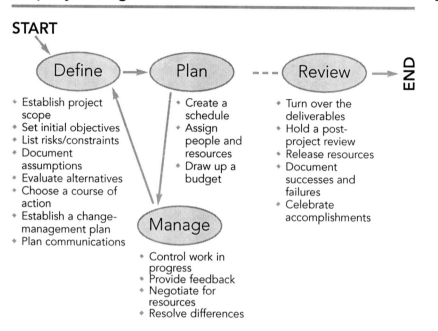

START

Define
* Establish project scope
* Set initial objectives
* List risks/constraints
* Document assumptions
* Evaluate alternatives
* Choose a course of action
* Establish a change-management plan
* Plan communications

Plan
* Create a schedule
* Assign people and resources
* Draw up a budget

Manage
* Control work in progress
* Provide feedback
* Negotiate for resources
* Resolve differences

Review
* Turn over the deliverables
* Hold a post-project review
* Release resources
* Document successes and failures
* Celebrate accomplishments

END

Note: If you'd like a free version of this model to teach to students working on projects in kindergarten through 12th grade, please contact us at info@russell-martin.com or www.russellmartin.com.

phase is no longer adequate. As the project progresses, unexpected glitches will test the manager's mettle. The arrows in figure 1.2 show you how Manage frequently tosses the project manager back into Define and Plan when it's done correctly.

4. **Review:** When the project is finished, it's not over. In this last phase of project management you *learn* from the project so that the next project goes even better. Although this phase often is skipped, it's a critical activity.

You'll learn more about the four phases of this project management model throughout the rest of the 10 steps.

Step 1 Checklist

   ✓ Determine which tasks on your to-do list are projects and treat them as such.

   ✓ Clarify the roles on your project team, including project manager, sponsor, and other stakeholders. Identify the people who will serve on your team.

   ✓ Help the project sponsor understand the role he or she will play on the project and how much time to reserve.

   ✓ Use the Dare Model as a checklist to ensure more thinking at the start of project and create more success at the end.

The Next Step

You have taken the first step—deciding if the activity you have at hand is a project. You've learned the basics of project management and clarified the roles. At this point, you're ready to move to Step 2, where you'll learn to clarify the business reason for the project—to prove your project is worth the time and effort that will be spent on it. That step is a critical prerequisite for creating your project plan.

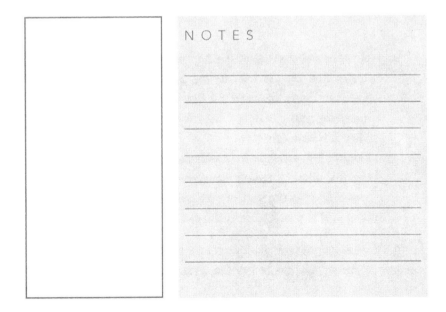

NOTES

Prove Your Project Is Worth Your Time

OVERVIEW

How Projects Are Financed

Your Sponsors and Your Stakeholders

Business Objectives— Underlying Reasons for Your Project

I once worked with a company that had plans to create a "corporate portal." It seemed like every time someone in the company asked for a new technical solution for a business issue or even a new report, the response was, "It will be in the portal." It became a running joke. No matter what question arose in a meeting, some smart aleck would say, "It'll be in the portal." When the technically quite sound portal actually materialized, it inevitably was met with disappointment from the business users because everyone had different expectations of it. You see, if people don't clearly understand what a project will deliver, they'll always be disappointed with what it does deliver.

Before a project can begin, it's critical to be as clear as possible on why you're doing the project. Whether in a business, a not-for-profit organization, or your personal life, many projects that change drastically in execution become troublesome because project sponsors

- didn't know they were sponsors, or didn't know what it meant to be sponsors.
- didn't agree at the start about how to measure the success of the project. In other words, they had different views about what the project would accomplish.

Catching

their breath, the three pigs slipped into a safe clearing behind a giant oak tree.

"Phew, that was close," said Speedy, the smallest and fastest pig. He already was able to speak *and* breath.

"Seems like that wolf gets closer every time," said his brother Demmy, carefully picking a grassy spot to sit down.

"Maybe I should have invested in a better pair of shoes," said Goldy, the third brother, looking sadly at his torn-up hooves.

"Clearly, we need to do something. We can't keep getting surprised and barely escaping with our lives day in and day out," said Speedy. "That wolf's out to get us, and he's making plans right now for our adventure tomorrow. We've got to do something, and fast."

Goldy looked up and glared. "Well," he said huffily, "we all agree we need a hiding place to protect us from him, but we waste time every day rehashing our differences on what kind of protection the house will get us. Here we are in this clearing, perfectly safe—and it's free. Seems to me that all your other fancy plans would spend useless dollars on building something that doesn't get us anything better than what we've discovered right here."

After a pause, Demmy spoke quietly. "We are safe here for now, but it's only a matter of time before the wolf discovers this spot, just like he discovered all the rest. When he comes here, we need to be ready. We need to think carefully about building a structure here that will protect us. We need to work secretively and take our time. Otherwise, if we're impulsive, we'll invest wasted effort and still we'll be in danger."

Each pig took a turn scowling at one another. They all bickered a bit more, and then each retreated to his own spot in the clearing. It was clear that each pig needed to build his own structure because they were never going to agree on just one.

Speedy gathered a pile of sticks and began hooking them together. Goldy picked up strands of straw and tied them together. Demmy, ever deliberate, set out on a walk into town to collect a load of bricks.

Clearly figuring out and recording why the entity is investing in a project is a critical first step. Building the "business case" for a project is not only answering the question, what will this project deliver? More important, it is answering the question, why do we need what this project will deliver?

The purpose of the project business case is to identify and write down (with the help or, at least, the review and agreement of the project's stakeholders) the reasons for the business to invest time and resources in the project. The business case includes the following components:

◆ the financial benefits to be produced by the completed project

◆ the expected costs entailed in completing the project

◆ the amount of time it will take to begin realizing benefits

◆ the requirements that must be met (revenue growth, service improvement, cost avoidance, regulatory compliance) to claim the desired benefits.

In this step you'll learn how project financials affect your project from beginning to end. You'll also learn how to ask the project sponsor the right questions to understand why the business is investing in this project.

Project Management Finances

Whether an organization is a for-profit or a nonprofit entity, its success requires a strategy. At least once a year, the leaders of a company should think about what changes to make during the next year to enlarge the success of their enterprise. They might think about new products or services to add, ways to lower

POINTER

Why Project Financials Matter

Clearly understanding the financials of a project helps the project manager

• understand how time delays or budget overruns will affect the financial status of the entire business

• prioritize different projects and identify which ones are most critical

• know when it's time to cancel a project that no longer makes financial sense.

costs, or changes needed to meet a regulatory requirement. A strategy is really an educated guess about how best to ensure survival and, ideally, growth.

When the leadership is in agreement, the strategy must be translated into action. At that point, projects are initiated. For example, if new products are to be added, then marketing plans have to be built, manufacturing has to be changed, and IT systems may need to be adapted. The success of these projects dictates how well the business is able to implement its strategy.

In a publicly traded company, business leaders publish projections about quarterly revenue. If those projections don't come true, the stock price usually falls. Ultimately, that makes it much more expensive for a company to do business. If a project's delay or failure is tied to a quarter's projected earnings, the firm's entire financial strength can be shaken by dropping stock prices. Few project managers understand this relationship.

Return-on-investment (ROI) is critical to a business. In our personal finances, too, we always want to make investments that return more than we started with. Here's the formula for calculating the ROI for a project:

Benefits generated by successful project completion
– Costs of doing the project
_____

Return-on-investment

Formulating project ROI starts with identifying anticipated benefits. Here are some typical project benefits:

◆ increased sales
◆ enhanced productivity (lower cost of goods sold)
◆ elevated quality (higher-end products)
◆ better service (greater customer loyalty)
◆ regulatory adherence and compliance (fewer fines and less litigation)
◆ increased market share and stock value.

The investment is the cost to do the project—software; hardware; IT experts; and people skilled in marketing, training, project management, and manufacturing. In most businesses today, information technology is one of the largest costs of strategic projects, and there are very few projects that contain no technical parts. Be careful, however, that you don't focus entirely on this investment aspect to the exclusion of all other costs. There are lots of costs in every project, and you need to track them all.

To produce a positive ROI—and therefore to make a project worth doing—the realized benefits must be greater than the costs involved. For this reason, a project that runs longer than was planned or requires more people to complete may become a project that doesn't produce the benefit required to justify doing it. Many project managers don't understand this way of looking at their project.

Project sponsors have the business focus, and their participation is critical in helping the project manager understand the ROI and monitor the project to know if the ROI still makes sense. The difference between a successful company and a struggling one is success at implementing good strategy through good project management.

Time to Complete This Step

When the information on anticipated benefits and likely costs has been gathered, it should take less than one hour to decide if the project is worth doing. How long it takes to gather the information will depend on how many stakeholders you have to ask.

Stakeholders

Every stakeholder should be involved in the initial business case discussion that you, as the project manager, should facilitate. This is the first chance you have to identify the stakeholders, and it may be the first time some of your stakeholders hear that they are stakeholders! As you read in Step 1, stakeholders are any people who have a vested interest in your project. Tool 2.1 lists potential stakeholders; use it as a checklist. To help you see project management practically applied, I'll use an imaginary blog project as a case study throughout the steps of this book, and example 2.1 shows you who are the stakeholders in that project.

Now let's get some practice identifying stakeholders by thinking about our three pigs. Read the portion of their story at the beginning of this step, and then turn to example 2.2.

TOOL 2.1

Potential Project Stakeholders

* People who provide you with information you need to do the project
* People who will use what the project produces
* People who have the authority to approve the project deliverables
* People who are investing money in the project
* People who have subject-matter expertise that you need
* People who have reason to know how the project is going
* People who will be on the project team

EXAMPLE 2.1

Blog Project Stakeholders

Scenario: A vice president of marketing for a software company has decided to fund the development of a blog where customers can exchange tips and get answers to frequently asked questions. He anticipates using Google Blog (free software) to create and host it. He's hoping to dedicate one person to building this blog (you) and one person to monitoring the blog for an hour a day when it's up and running.

In your role as project manager, you've developed this list of stakeholders:

* VP of marketing
* Google Blog help desk/tutorial
* person who'll monitor the blog
* customers
* IT/Web subject-matter experts

EXAMPLE 2.2

The Three Pigs' Stakeholders

Each pig is working on his own project, so each may have different stakeholders. List who you think the stakeholders are for each pig:

Speedy:

Goldy:

Demmy:

Answer: At first glance, it seems that two of them don't have stakeholders. Both Speedy and Goldy have enough free materials that they don't need to ask anyone else for help. But when you're listing stakeholders, it's better to consider all possibilities and include potential stakeholders. It's likely that each of the pigs will need the other two when building his home—especially to lift the roof sections. So, each pig has the other two pigs as stakeholders.

Demmy is looking for bricks, so he'll have to interact with others. Clearly, his list of stakeholders should include "people with bricks."

Finally, BB Wolf is a stakeholder for all three. He's really the reason for all three projects. The measure of success will be taken when BB finds the pigs and gets his huff on. A successful building will withstand the blast and protect its owner. Notice how critical this stakeholder is? Ultimately, the wolf is the final judge of the project's success, and in planning their projects, the pigs will do well to think carefully about the wolf and how he operates.

Questions to Ask

At this step in a project, you want to know why the business will be better off when this project is complete. To learn the reason(s), ask the following questions of the sponsors:

 ◆ How will completing this project increase the money (revenue) coming in?
 ◆ How will completing this project reduce the costs?
 ◆ How will completing this project improve the service provided to customers?

- How will completing this project grab market share from our competitors?
- How will completing this project meet the requirements of a new law or regulation?

The answers to these questions are called *business objectives*. Your project may be one of many that contribute to a specific business objective, but all projects need at least one business objective of their own.

Sometimes our personal projects really don't increase revenue, avoid cost, or improve service. Nonetheless, it's important to be specific about what amount of money and time you're willing to invest even for an aesthetic benefit. For example, if you're adding a deck on the back of your house, you'd ask yourself these questions:

- What will this deck bring me that I don't have now (perhaps a retreat, less stress, more room to entertain)?
- How much am I willing to pay to have these benefits?
- How much time am I willing spend to have these benefits?
- What other responsibilities do I have that I'm willing to put aside to add this deck?

Example 2.3 asks and answers the questions that fit our blog project.

Project Manager's Toolkit: Business Objectives

After you've collected the answers to your why-do-this questions, construct measurable business objectives and seek the agreement of your stakeholders about those objectives. You and the team will use the objectives to stay on track throughout the project.

EXAMPLE 2.3

Blog Project Business Objectives

Question: How will completing this project increase the revenue coming in?

Answer: The blog will be free to users and so will not directly affect our sales revenue. However, it will provide us with information about what features we need in our products to attract more customers and what product problems we need to address to keep the customers we have.

Question: How will completing this project reduce the costs?

Answer: Some of our Help Desk labor costs will be reduced when people are able to answer common questions themselves using the blog.

Question: How will completing this project improve the service provided for customers?

Answer: The blog will be a virtual discussion with our customers, enabling us to provide customized service quickly from our experts and from other customers who are experts.

Question: How will completing this project meet the requirements of a new law or regulation?

Answer: There is no regulatory need here. However, it is important that the identities of blog contributors be kept private and secure.

Question: How will completing this project grab market share from our competitors?

Answer: A web-based relationship with our customers will give us a presence on the web that our competitors don't have and will make us appear more technically savvy and responsive to customer needs.

Any project may have many business objectives, and each of them should be *measurable, achievable,* and *clear.* Here are a few examples from an array of businesses:

- Building this website will enable customers to place orders for our products from their offices and homes, which will increase our revenue 25 percent, according to recent market research.
- Replacing all the office windows with energy-saving windows will lower the company's monthly energy bill by $5,000.

◆ Training all of our people in more effective customer serv-ice techniques will make our stores more inviting to cus-tomers, and responses to our customer surveys will be 10 percent more positive.

◆ We will be HIPAA compliant and will avoid fines if we cre-ate forms for our patients to sign when they come in for their dental appointments.

◆ We will outmaneuver our fitness club competition by offer-ing a monthly pay-as-you-go package because our plans will attract customers who feel the competitors require contracts that are too long and costly.

Notice that each of the business objectives clearly states what is going to happen when the project is done and how the business will benefit. In a sense, by stating the objectives you are beginning to build the contract for the project. It's much more likely that a project will be successful at the end if you know at the start how success will be measured.

Also notice how most of those objectives have assumptions within them. For example, the fitness club's objective assumes that customers think other fit-ness centers charge too much and force them to commit to contracts that are too long. If that turns out to be a faulty assumption, the objective won't be met and the project will fail. As the project progresses, the proj-ect manager is likely to be the first person who sees signs that an underlying as-sumption is faulty, and his or her ability to react and adapt to such a discovery depends on a knowledge of the assumptions.

POINTER

A project done for regulatory or compliance reasons generally will have only costs and no benefits (beyond avoiding financial penalties and jail time).

You can practice defining business objectives for the three pigs' projects in example 2.4.

Communication

It's not possible for the project manager alone to answer the questions in this step. And on any project it's critical to ask all the stakeholders to think about measurable, achievable, and clear business objectives—your customers, web developers, network analysts, marketing managers, and so forth. If you're building a deck on the

EXAMPLE 2.4

The Three Pigs' Objectives

Here's how BB Wolf would answer your questions about the pigs' project objectives:

> *No way can those pigs build something to keep me from having ham for dinner! I'm three times their size, and I've got the strength to blow air so hard it can topple most things—except maybe rocks.*

With the wolf's perspective in mind, construct project objectives for each of the three pigs here.

Speedy:

Goldy:

Demmy:

Answer: Speedy has set the following project objective: *I'll build a house out of sticks so that I'm able to put it together very quickly. I'll hide inside it, and the wolf won't see me when he comes to eat me.*

Goldy has set the following project objective: *I'll build a house out of the straw in the clearing so that I'm able to construct it with very little cost. I'll hide inside the straw house, and the wolf will think it's just a pile tossed there by the farmers. He'll not find me when he comes to eat me.*

Demmy has set the following project objective: *I will search the area and get bricks so that I can build a strong house. The bricks will protect me from the wolf's big breath and he won't be able to eat me.*

back of your house, your partner, children, and friends will have thoughts that will prove very helpful early on. This step is the first opportunity you have to communicate with stakeholders, and communicating is a discipline that's crucial to project success.

If you're geographically unable to meet face-to-face with the sponsor, you may want to use conference calls or web meetings to make sure you have her or his full attention. The business objective discussion will always go better if you have a draft for the sponsor and other stakeholders to critique. The sponsor and stakeholders whose opinions matter at this point usually are high-ranking leaders with little time and insufficient focus for brainstorming types of discussions.

What If I Skip This Step?

If you avoid stating the business objectives, clarifying them, and gaining your stakeholders' agreement, or documenting them for the record, your project will struggle and probably fail. You'll begin building the project that you *think* the stakeholders want, instead of the project they *do* want. Without the boundaries defined by your objectives, you'll be tempted by every interesting thing that comes along because there's nothing to constrain you. Getting stakeholders involved here begins a communication pattern that will save you when glitches happen later in the project.

If your stakeholders avoid answering questions about the business objectives, watch out. That's a very bad sign and usually indicates the project is some executive's pet plan. Not a great career move over the long term. Continue to push for clear and measurable business objectives, and if you can't get consensus, document that.

Remember, it's the stakeholders who will judge the success of the project. The more perspectives you have answering the why-do-it questions at the very beginning, the more likely you'll reach a successful conclusion. If you're the only stakeholder, be clear in your own mind about what you want to accomplish.

Lurking Landmines

- *Your stakeholders really aren't sure what success will look like.* Stop the project, no matter how excited you are about it. There's no chance for success if the decision makers aren't clear about their reasons for investing in it.
- *Analysis paralysis sets in.* Project work can be a little intimidating, and sometimes we use any and all excuses to avoid starting and finishing. Don't spend too much time on this—ask the questions, build the objectives, get feedback and buy-in from the stakeholders, and move on.
- *There are no business objectives, but the big boss wants you to do it anyway.* Of course you'll do the project because the boss wants you to, but you'll start by clearly describing for the boss the risks involved. You'll also prepare for the rug to be pulled out from under you at a moment's notice, because this project eventually will be cancelled.

Step 2 Checklist

- ✓ Identify the stakeholders for your project.
- ✓ Create questions to find out why anyone/everyone wants to do this project.
- ✓ Work with the stakeholders to clarify the project's anticipated ROI, based on realistic time and money investments.
- ✓ Write all of this down and share the final list of business objectives with all stakeholders.

The Next Step

The next essential step will build on your list of stakeholders and the project objectives. You'll create a diagram to communicate the scope of the project to your stakeholders and team. When you've completed Step 2, everyone will know what project you're doing.

NOTES

Manage Scope Creep

We've all done it; in fact, I just did. Here I sit, determined to make some progress on this book, and I'm distracted by my email, a phone call, and all the intrigue happening at the coffee shop I'm visiting. Distraction is a kind of *scope creep*—easily succumbed to and difficult to avoid. With our mobile email and phones, we're in touch with everyone everywhere 24/7. It's always tempting to get pulled away by something new and exciting, or something old and ugly.

In project management, scope creep is the number-one killer of success. Inevitably, you'll start a project with certain parameters, and then it begins to grow, morphing into something bigger. This type of scope creep usually doesn't happen with a big decision or a loud confrontation; it happens quietly, one small concession at a time. Someone you like asks you to make a simple addition to your work that won't take you any time at all. Uh-huh. Before you know it, your tiny, simple project has become mission critical and due tomorrow.

Who creates scope creep? We all do. Project managers blame the stakeholders for changing their minds, but constant changes in business dictate that the stakeholders will have new requirements

In no time

at all, Speedy had finished his house. All that remained was a final inspection to see that he'd done everything he needed to do to protect himself. Sitting on his porch and tapping leftover sticks together, he noticed that different sticks made different, almost musical sounds. He had a wonderful idea—he'd get his brothers to form a band with him! All thoughts of his house and a final once-over flew out of his head as he turned his attention to gathering lots of unusual sticks to make new sounds and amaze his brothers. What a pity! If he'd paid more attention to his building, he'd have noticed that the top wasn't hooked into the four walls.

Meanwhile, Goldy ran out of straw—all the pieces he'd found on the ground had covered only half a house. He knew he could go to town and buy some straw, but that seemed extravagant. He wandered around, searching for things that would work like straw and not cost him anything. He gathered small pieces of paper, a tin can, a dead but leafy branch, and his favorite find—a giant piece of cardboard.

As Demmy went down the road to town, he stopped to talk with people he knew, asking their opinions about where to get the best bricks. With his friend Bob, he had a long talk about the history of brick as a building material, and they agreed it was important for Demmy to spend some time online researching types of brick before he chose his own. So off he went to the library.

throughout the project. Stakeholders blame project team developers—IT programmers who grow enamored of some fancy new technology that isn't really imperative, or graphic designers who spend additional hours unnecessarily tweaking cool animation. And, ironically, project managers can expand the scope by doing a good job of communicating because better information helps stakeholders think of factors they didn't consider before. And, you know what happens then.

Scope creep isn't a bad thing. But it must be managed. In fact, managing the change in scope as a project progresses is an important part of the manager's role. Scope will evolve continually. Many people have the impression that project management means controlling or eliminating scope creep—but that's completely wrong. If a project is going to continue to provide the business benefit detailed in the business objectives drafted and documented in Step 2, it has to evolve over time. If you could finish a project in several minutes or even a few days, you might have a fighting chance of starting and ending with the same scope, but most projects take much longer than that. And the longer the project takes, the more the scope will change, of course.

It does seem like I've just argued both sides of the scope creep dilemma—down with distractions and endless alterations and up with evolution! Here's the point. Scope creep kills a project only when the stakeholders, including the project manager, don't agree that the scope has changed. The big problem occurs when the scope has changed and the project sponsor doesn't think it has. The project team has more work to do but the sponsor expects it to be done with the resources originally assigned (time, people, and money).

Scope creep, when managed well, is a productive change process, ensuring that the project ultimately will meet the needs of the business. For everyone to be in agreement about what changes have been made and what the impact of these changes will be requires that

- the scope is defined and agreed to before the project starts
- any changes to the scope are added to the scope definition and agreed to before they are scheduled

◆ changes to the scope are reflected in realistic changes to deadlines, budget, and people time.

The business objectives, established in Step 2, help prioritize some of the scope changes. In this step, you'll create project objectives that are the criteria all will use to measure the final project results. As project manager, you'll use these project objectives as a contract with your stakeholders. But words on a page are not as meaningful as a picture, so here you'll also learn how to draw a picture of the scope so that scope communication is easier and everyone stays on the same page.

When you first meet with the sponsors and stakeholders, their natural focus will be on what they'll get when the project is complete. In a way, it doesn't matter to them who you'll have to work with to get to that point. The stakeholders are the people who provide you with the inputs you need and/or request something from the project. The scope of the project, then, is the point at which these inputs and outputs touch a stakeholder. Put another way, I can create a blog for an external customer to use, but within the scope of that blog-creating project, I can't make the customer use it. The stakeholders represent an imaginary set of fence panels around the project, and what is enclosed by those panels is the scope.

Time to Complete This Step

After you've gathered the information you need, expect to spend less than one hour writing the project objectives and one hour drawing the scope diagram. How long it takes to gather the information will depend on how many stakeholders you have to question. Bringing your stakeholders to consensus on the project objectives and scope diagram could take a significant amount of time, depending on how hard it is to get people to attend meetings or respond to email in your corporate culture. If the project really is needed by the sponsors, you should be able to get consensus on these within a couple of weeks.

Stakeholders

All stakeholders should be involved in the scope discussion if possible, facilitated by and including the project manager (you). Tool 3.1 shows the process I've found most useful for gaining stakeholder consensus about project objectives and the scope diagram. If you adopt this process early and use it regularly, it will teach the sponsors and stakeholders what you'll require from them throughout the project.

Questions to Ask

At this point, if you're working on a business-related project, ask the stakeholders Who will provide necessary guidance to the project team while we build the solution. Who are the subject-matter

TOOL 3.1

Steps to Gaining Consensus among Stakeholders

1. Research (without interviewing) any sources and materials that will help you create good, rigorous questions to ask when you meet with sponsors and stakeholders.

2. Meet individually with each sponsor and stakeholder, and ask your questions. Explain when you will send them a prototype of the project scope information, and by what date you would like to receive their revisions and suggestions.

3. Summarize the results of all your sponsor/stakeholder meetings and prototype the project scope information

4. Send your prototype to the sponsors and stakeholders, with a reminder of the return date.

5. Gather their responses—and nudge as needed to hit the dates you've specified.

6. If necessary, negotiate critical differences of opinion among sponsors and stakeholders.

7. Publish the project scope information with credit to each of the sponsors and stakeholders.

TOOL 3.2

Questions Concerning Project Inputs

1. Who will provide the requirements—that is, the specifications or details about what's ultimately needed at the completion of the project?

2. Who will be writing the check for the work? Who manages the project's budget?

3. Who will tell the project manager what processes or standards are to be followed?

4. Who will provide the technology needed?

5. Who will provide the people to work on the project, if needed?

6. Who will do the design work?

7. Who will do the testing or compliance work?

experts? Does one trump another? This information often is called the "project requirements," and it represents what I am calling one kind of "input" to the project. Sample questions to use in identifying the other types and sources of project inputs are offered in tool 3.2.

You'll also ask yourself, who or what will receive information and deliverables from this project? These "outputs" could be final products of the project but might also be interim information or prototypes developed as the project progresses. For example, it would be a good idea to send a list of the project objectives to the stakeholders for approval before moving along with the project—that list would be output. Tool 3.3 provides a few sample questions to help you describe and direct the outputs expected from your project.

Give It a Try

Try asking the *inputs* and *outputs* questions about one of the projects you're managing right now. What did you discover you hadn't thought of before?

To illustrate typical answers to questions posed in your search for input and output information, let's consider our blog project and ask the questions in tools 3.2 and 3.3. I've compiled a set of answers for you in example 3.1. At first glance, this project appears pretty simple, but as questions are raised, you can see in example 3.1 that there are very important things that aren't clear. For example, the question of how the blog will be transferred from the development team to the person monitoring it will be critical to successful implementation. No decision has been reached

TOOL 3.3

Questions Concerning Project Outputs

1. To whom will the project reports be delivered?

2. Who will receive the final project deliverables?

3. Are there any systems with which the project must build interfaces?

4. Who will do the training for the rollout when the project is completed, and what will they need to have for the training?

5. Who will handle marketing/sales for the rollout, and what will they need for that?

EXAMPLE 3.1

Blog Project Answers to Input and Output Questions

Project description: For our software development company, create a blog to answer customers' frequently asked questions.

Inputs:

1. *Who will provide the requirements—that is, the specifications or details about what's needed?*

   We will use Google Blog services. There is no pertinent expertise in the company, so we will learn how to do it through the Google Blog website.

2. *Who will be writing the check for the work? Who manages the project's budget?*

   The marketing VP has agreed to pay for 10 hours of one person's time to do this project, and to dedicate a person 1 hour per day to monitor this blog. There is no other budget money for this.

continued on next page

3. *Who will tell the project manager what processes or standards are to be followed?*

    We will use our normal time-tracking system to report actual hours spent on this project. No extraordinary processes or standards are required.

4. *Who will provide the technology needed?*

    We will use existing technology.

5. *Who will do the testing or compliance work?*

    The marketing VP will accept the final version of the blog. He will assign a staff member to do the final testing. There are no compliance issues.

Outputs:

1. *To whom will the project reports be delivered?*

    The marketing VP will receive usage statistics at the end of each week from the person monitoring the blog.

2. *Who will receive the final project deliverables?*

    The marketing VP and the person in charge of monitoring the blog will be taught how to view and maintain the blog.

3. *Who will do the training for the rollout when the project is completed, and what will they need to have for the training?*

    The project manager will do all development work, including the training mentioned above.

---

about who will have the final say on the finished products. People like to start projects on an agreeable note, so these types of pivotal questions often are avoided and neglected.

Let's return to our family deck-building project for a moment. Imagine how talking over the specifics of project inputs and outputs before the project begins will maintain harmony among all those involved. There will be fewer but similar inputs questions, and you'll notice that each primary question generates an additional, deeper question:

1. Who will provide the requirements of the project?

1a. Who decides how big the deck will be, what type of wood will be used, the final design?

2. Who will be writing the check for the work? Who manages the project budget?

   2a. Where will this money come from—cash? home equity loan?

3. Who will tell us what processes or standards are to be followed?

   3a. Are there times when the construction should not be done—at night? before what hour in the morning or on weekends? Will the garage be used to prep materials? For how long will that area be needed?

   3b. Do we need any permits? Where do we get them?

4. Who will provide the technology needed?

   4a. Will we need to buy/rent tools? What kind and where?

5. Who will provide labor?

   5a. Who will help us? How available are they?

And here are some pertinent outputs questions:

1. To whom will the project reports be delivered?

   1a. How will we measure progress?

Many relationships could be saved if couples used these kinds of simple questions to prompt a discussion before projects begin!

Project Manager's Toolkit: Project Objectives and Scope Diagram

Scope can be documented using the left (analytical) and right (visual) parts of your brain. In this step, you create project objectives (left brain) and a scope diagram (right brain).

Project Objectives

Project objectives are the written criteria against which a project's final deliverables are judged. They define how a finished project will be measured in terms of time, cost, and quality. Most projects have several or many objectives.

The most common guideline used for writing objectives of all kinds is the **SMART** approach. Tool 3.4 shows the characteristics of SMART objectives. You have asked the questions by this point and have lots of data from sponsors and other stakeholders to build your initial prototype of project objectives. Example 3.2 presents sample blog project objectives.

Scope Diagram

After you've collected the answers you need, you're ready to draw the picture. In that it focuses on where the project's boundaries are, a scope diagram is like a plat map of your property. Primarily, as with the questions asked earlier and the project objectives, the diagram helps you define for stakeholders the inputs and outputs the project will need to be successful. It also identifies which stakeholders will supply what inputs and which stakeholders will receive what outputs. Essentially, it clarifies everyone's responsibilities and expectations at the outset.

TOOL 3.4

Characteristics of SMART Project Objectives

* **S**pecific: The objective tells exactly what, where, and how the completeness of the project deliverable will be measured.

* **M**easurable: The objective states exactly how the project deliverable will be quantified—how much, how many, and how well.

* **A**ction-oriented: The objective uses "activity indicators" to ensure that something will be done. Use action-oriented verbs such as *deliver, implement, establish,* and *supply* to define how the project will present the expected results.

* **R**ealistic: The objective is a result that can be achieved in the time allowed and with the resources supplied.

* **T**ime-bound: The objective includes a specific date by which it must be achieved.

EXAMPLE 3.2

Blog Project Objectives

* A prototype blog website with 90 percent of all planned features and information will be available for testing 20 days before the launch date.

* The blog site will be hosted through the free service Google Blog so it will be available to customers 99.5 percent of the time.

* In a customer focus group, 80 percent of the customers surveyed will rate the usefulness of the site greater than 7 out of 10.

* All customer responses, comments, or other blog information will be monitored and proctored through an IT resource before being made available to other customers on the site.

* An email link for comments will be included at the bottom of each blog page, and all visitors who submit a comment via this link will receive a personal reply within one business day.

Let's use example 3.3 to illustrate a scope diagram. As we talk about how to read it, you'll be learning how to draw a diagram for your own project.

The rounded rectangle in the center is the project itself. Start there. It's too early really to know all the activities that will have to happen to get the project done, so at this point there's no detail about tasks inside that rectangle.

The squares surrounding the rectangle are the stakeholders. Every stakeholder identified for the blog project in Step 2 has his

---

POINTER

Artificial Project Objectives

Don't let creating project objectives become an academic exercise. Objectives don't take a lot of time to write, but it does take time to write them well. Avoid the temptation to show your brilliance by using big words that don't communicate fully, or by putting in artificial measurements (for example, *the customer will find the item he wants in 3.2 seconds*). It's *impossible* to make the objectives perfect this early in the project. Try to capture 80 percent of what the project will do and continue to update and develop the list as the scope changes.

EXAMPLE 3.3

Blog Project Scope Diagram

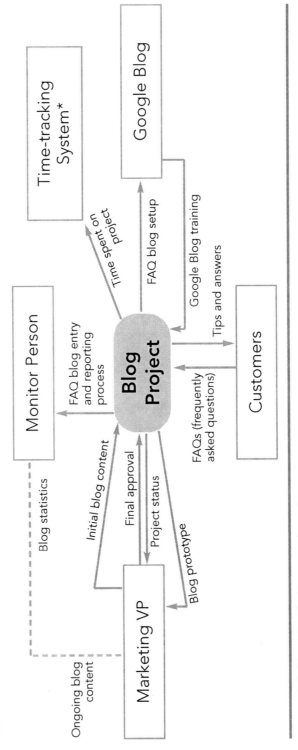

*New stakeholders identified in scope discussion.

or her own square on this diagram. That's also true of each person mentioned in the answers to questions asked earlier in this step. (*Note:* Be sure to add those people to your stakeholder list, too.) Notice that stakeholders are not only specific people. Sometimes the square may name a role or position (for example, marketing VP), a department or team (accounting), an external entity (Google Blog), or an application (time-tracking system).

Lines connect inputs from a stakeholder to the center rectangle, with arrows indicating the direction of flow. Likewise, lines connect project outputs to recipient stakeholders, with arrows showing the flow from the center rectangle to the receiving square. Each of the lines is labeled with the input or output flowing along it. When you construct your diagram, if you've already done more work on defining your objectives, you may want to use those objectives to draw the output arrows first. After that, look carefully at those output arrows and ask yourself, what else has to happen? That will prompt thoughts about other outputs and all of the inputs needed to produce them.

You'll have to make some decisions about *granularity*—what level of detail you show. You don't show every little input and output detail on this chart. For example, I try to avoid showing a request for information to a stakeholder (output); instead I prefer to show just the flow of the information back to the project (input). You're beginning to illustrate, at a high level, how your stakeholders will measure the success of the project. For example, "FAQ blog entry and reporting process" as an output to "Monitor Person" is a pretty general but important deliverable, and its arrow indicates a significant process handoff from the project team to the person who will monitor the website from implementation forward. There's going to be a lot to these process definitions that are transferred over, but at this point the label serves simply to show the significance of the Monitor Person as a stakeholder and to identify the type of flow to expect.

Here are some tips about drawing a scope diagram:
- ◆ Don't use double-headed arrows because it buries too much detail. It usually means you are showing that you've re-

quested something and received it. These actually are two different flows and, as mentioned earlier, it may be that it's not necessary to show the request. There is almost no chance that whatever is going from the stakeholder to the project will go back to the stakeholder unchanged. If it wasn't changed, why was it needed?

◆ Usually there are inputs from and outputs to the same stakeholder, but it is possible for a stakeholder to be only a supplier or a receiver (for example, a customer).

◆ Don't draw lines between stakeholders. As project manager, you can't monitor, control, or always know about flows between stakeholders, so don't try to document it. If you document it, you'll own it—and that creates scope creep. If illustrating such a flow is necessary to clarify some aspect of the project, show it with a dotted line rather than a solid line (as shown in example 3.3, from the marketing VP to the person doing the monitoring). This makes it clear that it takes place, but that it isn't in the scope of the project.

◆ Create the diagram on a flipchart page and carry it around to show people. Don't draw it on the computer (weird, huh?). When people see a beautiful computer picture, they don't think they can disagree with it, but people feel very comfortable changing something on a flipchart. It's better to know early what they're going to change.

Using your own project and worksheet 3.1 as a practice template, build a scope diagram. Share it with others who know what's involved in the project, preferably stakeholders. What do you learn in this activity that you never thought of before?

Communication

It's important that all stakeholders, especially project sponsors, review the project objectives and the scope diagram to ensure that they are accurate and complete. Avoid the temptation to email the objectives to your stakeholders. If they're busy, most people will agree without really reading them. Because, ideally, you're going to

WORKSHEET 3.1

Scope Diagram Template

Instructions: Use this template to create a scope diagram that illustrates the flows of inputs from and outputs to the stakeholders in your project. Connect the stakeholders (squares) and the project (rounded rectangle) with arrows pointing in the direction of flow. If necessary, use dotted lines to indicate flows between stakeholders.

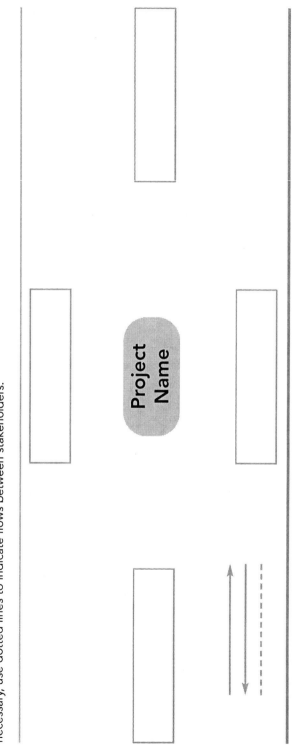

Project Name

be making in-person visits to present the scope diagram and explain its symbols, you might as well present the objectives at the same time. This kind of interaction provokes the most thoughtful exchange with stakeholders. In the real world, a brief meeting may not be possible, however, so here are a few ideas for getting the project objectives and the scope diagram validated:

◆ Create the project objectives prototype and distribute it through email for feedback. Use these objectives to draw a prototype scope diagram.

◆ Explain the scope diagram in a brief presentation. Walk the stakeholders through the diagram and get their feedback about its accuracy. Update the project objectives from this feedback

◆ When the scope diagram and the project objectives have been updated to reflect the stakeholders' feedback, send both documents out to the stakeholders for a final look.

Any changes to the scope should be added to the project objectives and the scope diagram, with the sponsors' permission. When added, new objectives will either be accompanied by more money or time, or will be accompanied by the removal of other project objectives they replace.

As we discussed earlier, novice project managers look for ways to freeze the scope of the project from the beginning. Your job is a lot easier if you can guarantee that the scope won't change, but *you can't*. Business doesn't work like that. Scope will change because business changes all the time. The diagram helps the project manager *manage* the

POINTER

Advantages of the Scope Diagram

• Pictures speak a thousand words. All stakeholders would rather review a picture with you than a document set in 10-point Times Roman.

• Drawing the inputs and outputs provokes new questions and new clarity.

• Sharing this graphic representation with stakeholders helps them better understand the complexity of the project.

• If you have multiple stakeholders, seeing the many flow lines helps them see why it isn't just all about their needs and their resources.

change; it doesn't help *refuse* the change. The stakeholders get to decide what stays and what goes, and this diagram facilitates that conversation.

Communication is the essential purpose of this diagram. As the scope changes throughout the project, this graphic representation can be adjusted so that everyone understands the choices that were made. It's an evolving element of the project.

You will realize the value of this scope diagram later in the project when, well down the road, someone suggests an additional requirement. If all the parties have seen and agreed to the scope diagram in the beginning, you, as the manager, have a tool to use in negotiating revisions in a nonconfrontational manner. Without the diagram, such discussions tend to become blame focused—"I told you it was in there; you just forgot it!" With this diagram you can help the stakeholder understand the impact of the change and make the best choices for the business.

What If I Skip This Step?

It's amazing how tempting it is not to clarify the scope. When I teach our project management simulations, it's very common for students not to ask when they don't understand the scope. When pressed, many people say they didn't have time to work out the scope. What they're saying is that is makes more sense to do a project wrong quickly than do it right with less of a jackrabbit start. Most stakeholders probably would not agree with that conclusion.

When we discuss the tendency not to ask or not to plumb a little deeper at the outset, most people confess that they're afraid they won't like the answer. That takes us right back to our Step 1 discussion about who owns the project. Not asking the questions, not considering the answers, not defining the boundaries lets you as project manager make the scope whatever you want until the project is about 80 percent done. If you haven't given them the chance before, suddenly the stakeholders tell you what they want and you're tossed into crisis mode, reorganizing and reworking. Remember, the sponsor owns the project and stakeholders define it. It's the stakeholders who will judge its success at the end. The more channels of communication you establish and travel in the beginning, the more likely it is that they'll get what they expect and be happy when the project is complete. Skipping this step is just shooting yourself in the foot.

The scope diagram also helps you jump-start some project work you'll be doing in future steps: For example,

- The more stakeholders (squares) you have, the more project risk you face because of increased communication. You'll use the information portrayed in the diagram to prepare for those risks and to build future communication plans.
- The diagram illustrates which stakeholders are most crucial to the project—they're the ones with the most arrows. Understanding their significance is a great help in building a communications plan.
- Each arrow represents at least one project activity (most likely, more than one). Realizing that will help you jump-start brainstorming the tasks for the project as you build a project schedule in Step 6.

Lurking Landmines

- *You ask too many questions and add scope to the project.* As you get the answers to your questions, keep comparing them to the original business objectives from Step 2. It's tempting to expand the scope of the project while defining it, but try to resist that temptation.
- *Different stakeholders want different things.* This diagram is great for showing all the stakeholders the full picture, so it's an asset when one stakeholder doesn't know what the other has asked for. Use your intuition—if it starts to feel like you're trying to do more than one project under the guise of a single project, use the diagram to question that approach. From a risk perspective, two tightly focused projects have more chance of success than one large, vague project.

Step 3 Checklist

    ✓ Ask good questions and create a list of project objectives.

    ✓ Identify the sources of the inputs to your project.

    ✓ Identify the recipients of the project outputs.

    ✓ Draw a scope diagram showing stakeholders, inputs, and outputs.

    ✓ Review project objectives and scope with all stakeholders, revising them until you achieve consensus (or at least compromise).

The Next Step

In the next step, you'll learn how to predict the project risks and build contingency plans to meet them. When you've completed the work of Step 4, you'll be ready to start the project.

NOTES

Identify, Rate, and Manage Risks

STEP **4**

We like to think that we're clairvoyant when it comes to project management. Any truly talented professional (and we all are, of course) *should* be able to plan and estimate a project accurately. It's our responsibility as project managers to anticipate every possible problem that might come up. After all, we've been managing projects for years, and we've been fairly successful.

Well, the truth is that every project will surprise you and on every project unexpected things will happen. It's irrational to think you can know everything before you know anything (that is, at the beginning). Glitches happen. Think of the last project you were on. What things occurred that you never expected? What impact did they have on your project throughput?

Although you can't anticipate the myriad challenges that will pummel your projects, you can look at the environment the project will start in and make some educated guesses. Doing so helps you begin to identify those "perfect storm" surprises that may occur and enables you to do some contingency planning. In this step you'll learn

While Speedy

collected the perfect sticks to outfit his new band, he felt worry creeping up on him. Maybe he had underestimated the wolf, as his brother had said. Maybe the stick strategy wouldn't work.

"Phooey," he said, pushing out the worries. "It's a good bet that BB Wolf has moved on to other towns by now, and that this whole building project is a complete waste of time." And he turned again to his musical stick search.

Goldy, too, was taking another look at his building plan. He'd used the bits of paper, the tin can, the dead branch and its crispy leaves, but when he'd wiggled the cardboard into position, the whole house had collapsed! Goldy was getting very irritated with the whole project, and he let loose a great sigh. Then he started again—building the same structure with the same materials. Tired and dispirited, he lost track of time and almost completely forgot why he was doing this work.

In town, the library lights were on. Demmy realized that it would be dark in less than an hour and he still needed to buy some bricks and get to building before night fell. Lost in his research, he really hadn't left himself enough time. He ran to the store and made a fast purchase. But, standing beside the stacks of baked clay, he had no idea how he was going to get all those bricks back to the site. He had a little money left and he bought a wagon, knowing it would take a long time to drag that loaded wagon back to the clearing. Slowly moving up the road away from town, Demmy thought about his troubles—his fear that the wolf might show up at any moment, his fear that the bricks wouldn't be strong enough to stop the wolf, and his fear for the safety of his two brothers.

what *risk* is. We'll cover techniques for analyzing a project's risk before the project starts and for building plans to counteract problems that pop up. We'll also ask the stakeholders to define the constraints of the project—in other words, rank the importance of timeline, budget, quality, and scope. These constraints give us clues to what might be the most detrimental risks. For example, if a project has a limited budget, running out of money will be a very serious risk.

There is a psychological advantage to thinking about risks and constraints before the project starts. Remember, it's much easier to react to a project glitch when you've already thought out how to handle it. Surprises, especially bad ones, get our attention too late because we really don't want to see them.

What Are Risk and Risk Management?

A project risk is an uncertain event that can affect the timing and completion of project objectives. A risk can occur at any time in the project; and when it occurs, it can alter the business objectives, the project objectives, the scope, and development work that's already completed.

Consider our blog project. There's a risk that creating the Frequently Asked Questions area might require help from subject-matter experts who aren't available when the developer needs them. If that happens, the project will be delivered later than expected. By identifying this risk up front, the project manager can clarify with sponsors and other stakeholders that making those experts available when the project schedule demands their help will be critical to on-time completion. That's *risk management*.

Risk management is not about controlling or eliminating risk. It's about anticipating it and planning ways to manage it without destroying the project. The process of risk management comprises the five steps shown in figure 4.1.

Notice that the first four steps—identify, analyze, prioritize, and plan—happen during the **Define** phase of project management,

FIGURE 4.1

Five-Step Process for Managing Risk

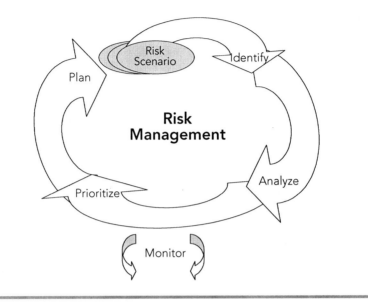

which is at the very beginning of a project (refer to figure 1.2). But it's likely that some risks will not be discovered at the start, so a successful project manager stays on the lookout for new risk factors —which is the last step, monitoring. Here's what happens in the five steps:

1. **Risk identification** happens during the initial project brainstorming and question-asking sessions. It involves defining potential problems in general terms.

2. **Risk analysis** involves uncovering enough of the details regarding a risk to be able to determine its impact on the project and the likelihood that the risk will occur.

3. **Risk prioritization** is a process to rank potential problems according to their potential impact and the probability of their occurring.

4. **Risk planning** defines both proactive and reactive project activities either to avoid (best case) or to mitigate (worst case) possible problems.

5. **Risk monitoring** reinforces the importance of always looking for additional risks that have not been identified, no matter what phase of the project you're in. Actually, this is psychologically pretty tough—no one wants to see a risk; and the closer the project comes to the end, the less a project manager wants to find out about a new risk.

Good risk management brings with it the following benefits:

◆ It minimizes "management by crisis."
◆ It anticipates risk as early as possible in the project.
◆ It helps a project manager determine how much time to spend planning, organizing, and controlling the project. The higher the risk, the more time is spent on project management, and the more formal the communication with the stakeholders becomes.
◆ It contributes to a shared project vision.
◆ It keeps the project focused on the business objectives.

In this step, you first identify the overall risk of the project as a whole. This quick-and-dirty risk assessment will help you weigh how important risk management is for your project. Obviously, a project that presents a lower level of risk doesn't need as much contingency planning as does a high-risk project.

After identifying the overall risk, you'll identify, analyze, prioritize, and plan what to do about individual risks. As you get consensus from the stakeholders about the project constraints (time, cost, quality, and scope), you'll begin to see which risks are the most important. Finally, you'll plan to monitor risk throughout the project.

Time to Complete This Step

Documenting risk is not time consuming (an hour should be fine), but brainstorming effectively does require some time away from constant interruptions. Ask the needed questions of the stakeholders, and then dedicate at least a couple of hours with your team to think creatively about what could go wrong and how you might address those things.

POINTER

Risk management is
a continuous activity.
Although the process
begins at the earliest
point of project
planning, risk itself
can occur at any
time. A good project
manager knows how
to watch for risk and
act swiftly to mitigate
it to keep it from
undoing all the good
project work that has
been done.

Stakeholders

In the ideal situation, all stakeholders are
involved in the discussion of risk and constraints facilitated by and including you as
the project manager. More likely, you'll do
the analysis yourself and share it with the
stakeholders for their feedback. Be warned
that risk is not something people like to
think about. It's natural to want to start a
new project with total optimism. The last
thing the stakeholders want to talk about
is what might happen to damage their
project and their reputation. Continue to
persuade them by stressing the proactive
importance of risk identification.

It's highly unlikely that the stakeholders will identify the risks
clearly for you. Instead, you'll take what you've learned from them
and identify the risks by using

- your brain, creativity, and intuition/inner voice
- business objectives
- project objectives
- project scope
- budget
- known and unknown business requirements
- schedule and deadlines
- lessons learned in past projects.

Questions to Ask

The best asset you have in managing risk on a project is your intuition. Given enough focus, a project manager can learn to trust that
inner voice that tries desperately to get attention. I've grown aware
of how my intuition wakes up quickly while I'm talking to a project
stakeholder. I don't always take the time to listen right then, but

TOOL 4.1

Questions Concerning Project Risk

1. What have I heard people say that my intuition tells me implies future problems?

2. What has surprised me in the past on projects similar to this one?

3. What are some of the challenges I've had in the past working with these stakeholders?

4. Is there organizational friction between the functional areas that will make it difficult to reach consensus among the stakeholders?

5. Considering the following factors, what can I imagine might happen to stall the project?
    People—stakeholders, vendors, project team, me
    Process, standards
    Technology
    Incentive, measurements
    Politics, organizational changes
    Training
    Shared resources
    Funding, budget
    Scope
    The economy—local, national, global

at least I've started to notice. After many projects, I'm convinced it's not the knowns but the unknowns that cause projects to fail.

At this point in your project, whether it's business or personal, ask yourself, what are some of the things that might happen to mess this up? These are the project risks. Tool 4.1 offers some questions you can ask yourself and your stakeholders.

In addition to identifying the possible risks, it's important to get consensus around the priorities of the project. As project manager, your job is to deliver the preestablished project objectives (as you read in Step 3) regarding

◆ the time the project will take
◆ the budget
◆ the quality of the project deliverables
◆ the scope.

These four factors are called the constraints of the project, and you will learn how to document them in a matrix toward the end of this step.

Project Manager's Toolkit: Handling Risk and Constraints

After you've collected the answers to your questions, you're ready to

- quantify the risk inherent in the project—the likelihood of failure—by identifying the areas of weakness
- create proactive and reactive contingency plans for high-impact glitches
- prepare a graphic to show the prioritization of constraints at the start of the project so you can communicate effectively when these priorities change during the project.

Here are some of the advantages of the tools and activities discussed below:

- The quick-and-dirty risk assessment takes only five minutes to discover how risky your pending project really is; how well the stakeholders understand the risks; and how much time you'll need to commit specifically to organizing, managing, and controlling the project.
- The risk management process, including the risk scenario you'll draft, helps stakeholders and project team members adopt realistic expectations about a project before it starts. It takes off the blinders and makes the inevitable glitches and occasional serious problems more psychologically acceptable. This keeps the project from spinning out of control from surprise and denial.
- The constraints matrix you'll construct helps you identify what options you have when the project doesn't go as planned. It keeps you from trying to negotiate project factors on which the sponsor is unwilling to budge. It also helps the stakeholders get some clarity around how they'll measure the success of their project, given the constraints it faces.

Quick-and-Dirty Risk Assessment

Worksheet 4.1 uses three project factors as risk criteria to assess the principal areas of risk in a project—size, structure, and technology. Stakeholders, project team members, and the project manager rate each criterion *relative to other projects he or she has been*

WORKSHEET 4.1

Quick-and-Dirty Risk Assessment

Instructions: Use these three ratings to think about this unique project. Rate each risk relative to the project team's experience, not the company's experience. For example, if the project will use an older technology, such as PowerPoint software, but the project team members have never used PowerPoint, the applicable technology would be rated as a higher risk. When each of the three ratings is complete, average them by adding the three criteria scores and dividing by 3. That average is your project's risk assessment score.

Risk Criterion 1:
Project Size: How "big" is this project or how long will it take?

1	2	3	4	5	6	7	8	9	10
SMALL/SHORT									LARGE/LONG

Risk Criterion 2:
Project Structure: Considering the following reasons why project requirements are or may become less stable, how stable are your project's requirements?

* There are no available subject-matter experts.

* Project requirements are tied to a government regulation that is changing or hasn't been defined fully.

* The project involves stakeholders and subject-matter experts with completely different opinions about the requirements. The more stakeholders there are or the more they argue, the more difficult it will be to define the requirements.

1	2	3	4	5	6	7	8	9	10
FIXED									UNDEFINED

Risk Criterion 3:
Applicable Technology: How well does the project team understand the technology?

1	2	3	4	5	6	7	8	9	10
EXPERIENCED									INEXPERIENCED

associated with in the past. For example, if I'm part of the blog project team and I have no idea what a blog is, I'm going to see the technology question as an area of greater risk than is someone who's worked with blogs a great deal.

The first criterion, *size*, specifies how extensive the project is in terms of the quantity and size of its deliverables and the length of time it will take. Remember, responses should be relative to earlier projects. Think about the amount of work involved when you rate this. Large, lengthy projects create risk factors that smaller projects do not—for example, staff turnover, communication difficulties arising from the great number of stakeholders, and budget amounts that are difficult to manage.

The second criterion, *structure*, focuses on the number of stakeholders and the delineation of specifications. The greater the number of stakeholders and/or the less certain and stable the specifications, the higher the risk of unclear requirements. For example, during the implementation of an enterprise-wide software system, the project manager will get requirements from executives responsible for every functional area. It's very normal for the different functional leaders to disagree on project priorities. In smaller projects completed within one business area, it's less likely that the requirements will be so confused by disagreement.

The third risk criterion, *technology*, is evaluated by rating the project team's familiarity with and ability to use the pertinent technology. We've all been victims of new technology. It's hard to estimate how long it will take to become proficient in the technology, and it's possible that the features of the technology may differ from what was advertised or contracted.

The most effective way to use this worksheet is to have all the responders individually rate the three risk factors and average their three scores. If the worksheet is used at a group meeting, ask each participant to share her or his score with the group. Interesting conversations come from the stakeholders interpreting the three questions differently. Facilitate this discussion until the group is able to agree on a rank for each criterion. It is important that all people involved start the project with the same perception of risk for the project.

Here are some things to talk about with the stakeholders as you discuss their quick-and-dirty worksheet scores:

◆ If the project comes out with an overall score of 3 or less, it's probably OK to wing it. Some projects just don't need a lot of attention.

◆ If the project comes out greater than 5, you as project manager will need to hold time periodically to think about your project. When the risk is lower, it probably isn't necessary to schedule "thinking," but for higher-risk projects you tend to get too busy to step back from the details and look at the big picture.

◆ If the risk consensus is 9 or 10, the project is in big trouble. It's highly unlikely that the project will be successful. Look for ways to break the large project into smaller ones that will isolate risks and be easier to manage.

As a project manager, you learn a great deal from this overall risk score. This number will help you define the amount of time you'll need to dedicate to managing the project, especially if you're both the project manager and the entire team. The higher this number, the more time you'll spend on managing activities because higher-risk projects will require more communication, negotiation, conflict resolution, and politicking to work around and through the glitches. Tool 4.2 will help you anticipate and allocate the needed management time that the quick-and-dirty assessment suggests.

TOOL 4.2

Amount of Time Needed for Project Management, Based on Anticipated Risks

Quick-and-Dirty Overall Risk Score	Management Time
1–4	10 percent of the time you spend on the project each week (for example, 4 hours if you spend 40 hours a week on the activities of this project)
5–7	15 percent of the time you spend on the project each week
8–9	2 hours a day
10	25 percent of the time you spend on the project each day (for example, 2 hours in an 8-hour day spent on the project)

STEP **4**

If the assessed risk of your project is 5 or greater, continue to the next item in this toolkit—the risk scenarios. (There are some people who recommend building risk scenarios regardless of the score, but you can decide when further analysis is merited. Trust your intuition.)

Remember that this number represents a point in time. If any of these three factors change as the project progresses, reintroduce the worksheet to stimulate another stakeholder discussion about why the numbers are no longer accurate and what you can do about it.

Don't be tempted to compare the quick-and-dirty risk numbers to those of other projects, especially with different teams and stakeholders. Risk scores on your project reflect the assessments of the people involved with your project. The assessment pertains to your stakeholders as the situation exists at the moment, and it's useful only for prioritizing the work of the project for which it was done.

Risk Scenarios

One way to facilitate thinking about risk is to gather a group of people to tell stories. These stories are brief descriptions of situations that could occur in the future and would hinder the project. By sharing these stories, called *risk scenarios,* you essentially complete the first two steps of the risk management process: identify and analyze.

Identifying Risks

Using answers to the questions at the beginning of this step, you're ready to tell a story to identify and thoroughly describe each risk by documenting

1. how the risk will affect the success of the project
2. how the risk will affect the business.

Here's an example of a risk scenario from the blog project:

> What would happen if the chief information officer (CIO), who is the sponsor of this project, was replaced in the middle of the project with a new CIO? We think that the project would come suddenly to a halt. Our current CIO sees this project as a strategic imperative to improving the effectiveness of the information technology area, but a new CIO might want to move in a completely different direction.

The risk identified through this scenario is the risk that the CIO will leave in the middle of the project. The story adds the details to make the experience real to the people discussing it.

Analyzing Risks

Risk analysis is the process of dissecting potential risks, analyzing their probability in a given set of circumstances, and envisioning their impact. In this step, you'll take each scenario, drill down into the specifics of the problem, and then determine the impact on the project and the probability that this risk will occur. "Impact" here means how detrimental to the success of the project the risk would be if it were to occur. For example, the risk of the CIO leaving could stop the project in its tracks, so it would be rated as high impact. The risk of a project team member missing a lot of work might have less of an impact and so be rated low or medium, especially if the project manager plans for cross-training.

In general terms, a low-impact risk will negatively affect cost, schedule, and quality by 5–10 percent; a medium-impact risk will negatively affect those factors by 10–15 percent; and a high-impact risk will produce upward of a 20 percent negative change in those factors.

Next, ask the stakeholders to help you judge the probability that a risk will occur. A low probability means that stakeholders believe the risk has less than a 25 percent chance of occurring. Medium probability means that the risk has a 25–60 percent chance of happening. High-probability risks are likely to occur in at least 60 percent of cases. Again, using our scenario example, the question would be, How likely do you think it is that the CIO will be replaced? If it's 60 percent or more likely, it's a high-probability risk.

Prioritizing Risks

Tool 4.3 shows you how to use a risk's assessed impact and probability levels (determined in the last section) to prioritize the risks of your project, which will help you communicate to your stakeholders the additional time and resources you'll need to handle these potential risks. Obviously, prioritizing is a more time-consuming process than simply listing the possible risks, but prioritization is the key to effective risk management. In larger projects, there is only enough time to deal with the most serious risks. Even in smaller projects, project managers have to balance the time it takes to avoid risks with the cost of adding this overhead to the project.

Please notice that although the impact and probability analyses use numbers, the project manager and stakeholders really are making educated guesses, not statistical choices. These numbers can't be compared with the numbers for another project—it would make no sense. The ratings of high, medium, and low for impact and probability help rank risks *within* a project but do not apply when prioritizing risks across different projects.

Planning for Risks

Not only does tool 4.3 show the priorities of the risks by ranking their impact and probability, but it also recommends three appropriate

TOOL 4.3

Prioritizing Risks

Probability

		Low	Medium	High
Impact	Low	Monitor	Monitor	Contingency
	Medium	Monitor	Contingency	Mitigate
	High	Contingency	Mitigate	Mitigate

Monitor: Keep an eye on the risk, but don't build any plans for contingency
Contingency: Build high-level contingency plans to implement if the risk occurs
Mitigate: Build plans to avoid and react to the risk

actions for different urgency/probability combinations—monitoring the risk, making contingency plans, and mitigating the risk.

When you make contingency plans, you monitor more frequently and add tasks to your project schedule to take proactive action to avoid the risk. In mitigating a risk, you build detailed plans to avoid the risk or soften its impact.

In the tool, notice that the low-impact risks demand the least attention, and high-impact risks require the most. The middle ground is interesting: a high-probability/low-impact risk has a slightly higher priority than other low-impact risks, primarily because it's more likely to occur.

At this point it's time to build a risk mitigation plan for the risks that fall into the contingency planning and mitigation planning

The Mystery of Probability

Academically, risk assessment treats impact and probability as relative equals when prioritizing risks and planning mitigation. With my experience, I weigh impact higher than probability. In fact, I've been burned on projects when I convinced myself that the probability was low and stopped monitoring.

areas of tool 4.3. For contingency planning, document obvious steps you can take to avoid the risk (these are tasks you will add to your project plan in Step 6) and high-level actions to take if the risk occurs. For risks that must be mitigated, document detailed steps to avoid the risk, if possible, and detailed plans for addressing the risk if it occurs. Both will add tasks to your project plan in Step 6.

Example 4.1 presents sample plans for mitigating risks associated with our blog project. Here are some additional issues to watch out for as you apply risk management to your project:

◆ People don't like to sit around at the beginning of a project and imagine all the things that might go wrong. Most prefer to stay in project nirvana, at least until the project starts. Facilitate the difficult conversations and don't let the stakeholders avoid them.

◆ Each contingency plan adds tasks (costs, time) to your project. Spending project time on risks that don't need detailed mitigation planning is bad for your project. It's possible to overdo risk management and take away valuable time from the project's implementation.

◆ This is not an academic exercise. Whatever mitigation tasks you document also will appear in your project plan for high-impact/high-probability risks.

Monitoring Risks

Once the project moves into the **Manage** phase, a project manger uses the risk prioritization matrix and risk tasks in the project schedule to monitor the project risk. If new project risks occur, the project manager revisits the risk analysis, definition, prioritization, and management steps above.

EXAMPLE 4.1

Blog Project Risk Mitigation Plans

Risk Factor	Avoid Risk	React to Risk
Project sponsor leaves the company	Communicate with other executives who might become the project sponsor	Meet with the new project sponsor and review the work done in Steps 2 and 3
Project is cancelled	Keep the project focused on the return-on-investment/business case, and communicate it to all stakeholders	Carefully document the ending, put all pertinent materials in a box, and move on
The technology doesn't work as planned	Investigate alternative technologies; choose technology that is more familiar to us	Be prepared to use less-risky technology if necessary; reduce the complexity of the soft-ware features needed

Constraints

Tool 4.4 presents questions to ask the stakeholders to discover their priorities relative to possible future problems. The questions will help you identify, at a macro level, the project's current constraints. This will help you communicate more effectively when project priorities change. The risks are things that you do *not* want to have happen. The project constraints are the factors that you *do want the project to deliver* to be successful. For example, one of the constraints of a project could be its completion date—it has to be finished by the end of the year because of a pending government regulation. Time is an important project constraint in that case. One of the highest-impact risks on such a project naturally would be something that put the project behind schedule.

Identifying the project constraints after the risk mitigation plans have been constructed provides an audit to make sure that nothing has been missed. It's a fairly difficult conversation for stakeholders to agree to the constraints of the project, and after

TOOL 4.4

Questions Concerning the Project Constraints

1. If the project was struggling, how much more time could we get?

2. If the project was struggling, how much more money would be available?

3. If the project was struggling, what project objectives could be delayed until a future release?

4. What would be the impact if we delivered the project with less-than-perfect quality?

getting through the risks there should be enough trust to get to consensus.

Worksheet 4.2 shows a blank matrix you can use to communicate the constraints of a project. Ask each stakeholder to indicate the most important constraint of the project by drawing an "X" in the column marked #1. The questions in tool 4.4 help you gain insight to the real constraints of the project. Using our example of the project time constrained by pending government regulations, one way to test that time is really the #1 priority is to request an extension on the deadline. If the deadline can be moved, then time is not the #1 priority.

Here's the rule: There can only be one "X" in each column and row—in other words, no two factors can have the same priority. It's possible, however, for #1 and #2 to be extremely close together and practically not negotiable.

Consider the U.S. project to put a man on the moon by the end of the 1960s. What was the #1 constraint of that project? Many people would say time because there was extreme social and political pressure to beat the Soviets to the moon. By putting time as #1, quality must move down to either #2 or #3. Clearly, the goals of the project wouldn't be met if the astronauts didn't survive because quality was sacrificed in the service of time. Here's how the moon project was prioritized:

- ◆ #1 quality (bring the astronauts back alive)
- ◆ #2 time (beat the Soviets)
- ◆ #3 cost (whatever it takes).

Let's return to the government regulation project. Imagine that two different areas of the company are involved in financing this project. One of the areas needs the project done in time to meet the government regulation, but the other needs the project done to roll out an important new product on the market. One project-customer rates time #1, but the other rates quality #1. It's unlikely that the project will successfully satisfy either stakeholder if this core difference cannot be resolved early on.

Example 4.2 shows the constraints of our blog project. Time is #1, followed in order by cost and quality. At first glance this seems inappropriate. The marketing vice president is anxious to get help for the customers, so time is most important. There is a limited budget for this, and that's why the company wants to leverage free software services (Google Blog). Because the blog faces the customer, quality has to be important, so why would a business knowingly invest in a project with the plan to neglect quality as a way of finishing inexpensively and on time? This is where scope comes in.

If a project has limited funds and needs to be done fairly quickly to get market share, as the blog project does, there are only two choices of mitigating action to take when a risk threatens to drive up the cost or slow down the project: (1) no changes are

WORKSHEET 4.2

Constraint Priorities

Constraint	#1	#2	#3
Time			
Cost			
Quality or Scope			

EXAMPLE 4.2

Blog Project Constraints

Constraint	#1	#2	#3
Time	X		
Cost		X	
Quality or Scope			X

made to the project size (that is, its scope) and the project is implemented poorly (with bad quality) or (2) the scope is reduced so that a smaller version of the project can be delivered at an acceptable level of quality. That's why scope and quality are combined as the third category in the constraints matrix.

The important point is that the matrix shows that scope is an important negotiation element for a project manager. When time and cost are threatened, as often happens, a project manager must negotiate scope or the quality will suffer through neglect. You documented scope and secured stakeholder consensus in Step 3 because you can't negotiate scope as a risk management strategy if the stakeholders haven't agreed already to your depiction of scope.

Try filling out worksheet 4.2 for one of your projects. Remember—only one #1, one #2, and one #3 priority. Keep these options in mind when you raise the following questions with your stakeholders:

- If I'm running out of time, would I be able to get more time? If not, would I be more likely to get more resources or to have to narrow the scope?
- If I've run out of money, would I be able to get more? If not, would I be more likely to get additional time or to have to cut the scope?
- If I realize that the scope of the project is too large to finish on time and within budget, can I get more resources or

time? Will I be able to reduce the scope and deliver a smaller amount of the project on time and within budget?

As the project progresses, here are two situations to watch for:

◆ Constraint #3 often becomes #1 because it's been neglected and has gotten out of control. Suddenly, it becomes the conflict point. For example, if scope is #3 in our blog project, somewhere down the road the marketing VP will start screaming about the lack of functionality being provided for the money. The original matrix can be used to remind the VP of why the compromises were made. If the priorities do need to change, create a changed matrix to go forward.

◆ Priorities change. Because the constraints matrix is a living document, it's important that you update the priorities when they change and make sure that all stakeholders agree to the new order.

Given your project challenges, as project manager you have three things to negotiate with the project sponsor as risks occur: time, cost, and scope. You'll negotiate these elements throughout the life of the project. The priorities will change over time, especially as deadlines approach and budgets are tapped. Scope is often the only factor that you reasonably can negotiate and still have the project be successful.

Communication

Again, the sole purpose for doing the quick-and-dirty risk assessment, developing a risk scenario, making plans to monitor or manage risks, and prioritizing constraints is to communicate. Risks and constraints change as projects proceed, so use those tools to build ongoing communication with the stakeholders. The risk plans will help you react quickly to problems and will enable you to tell the stakeholders what has occurred and what you intend to do about it. The constraint matrix will help you communicate with the sponsors when the priorities of the project seem to have changed.

When a change does occur, everybody will know that it has, and the owners of the project (the sponsors) can reach agreement about the best course of action. In Step 7, you'll learn how to manage and negotiate project change.

What If I Skip This Step?

Don't. The activities in this step take very little time and will have a huge effect on how you prepare your project plan estimates and tasks. If you don't do your risk analysis and management planning now, you will spend more time dealing with problems when the project is in progress.

Take the time to anticipate and prepare for risk and to communicate with everyone connected to the project exactly how profound the risks may be and specifically what plans you've made to manage problems that may arise. At the end it is the stakeholders who will judge the success of the project. The more information you communicate in the run-up to the project, the more likely they are to be happy when the project is complete.

Lurking Landmines

◆ *Different stakeholders prioritize constraints differently.* It's highly unlikely that all stakeholders will be happy at the end. They come from different areas inside and outside the organization, and each wants something that fully satisfies his or her own priorities. The key to producing outcomes that everyone finds successful is in building consensus and trust among stakeholders and sponsors. Making space and opportunity for everyone to discuss risks together creates a shared choice of the appropriate actions to take and acceptable trade-offs to make if/when specific problems arise. Moving the discussion up the line to a project sponsor may be necessary when stakeholder agreement is out of reach. Don't delay that movement.

◆ *The sponsor may want it all—every aspect of the project scope, on time, within budget, and at top quality.* Don't agree to fantasy, and don't take no for an answer when you ask a sponsor to agree to some reasonable concessions to save a project. Instead of asking the sponsor to pick an aspect to sacrifice—time, budget, or scope/quality—ask questions that prompt the sponsor to describe what he or she really would do if the project began to struggle for one reason or another. Help the sponsor hear his or her own priorities revealed in those answers.

Step 4 Checklist

✓ Identify the overall risk of the project.
✓ Describe the likely high-impact risk scenarios and build proactive and reactive mitigation strategies.
✓ Identify the order in which your stakeholders and sponsors prioritize the project's constraints.
✓ Create a habit of consensus and communication with the stakeholders.

The Next Step

In the next step we'll discuss how to influence the most unpredictable factor in any project—the people involved. You'll learn how to identify and adapt to people's unique communication styles and their diverse motivations. Essentially, you'll learn how to lead a project and how to manage its politics.

STEP **4**

Collaborate Successfully

STEP **5**

My company worked on a large training roll-out for state agencies getting new software. As our project team developed the training, they often were irritated by the software developers' inability to get them the screens, reports, and basic application functionality that the training was supposed to teach. Each morning a different course developer would remark about what jerks the software people were. When classes began, the trainers often were furious to find that the programmers hadn't reset the test data or had changed another screen during class! Rarely did a day go by that someone wasn't mad at a software company staff member.

I'm guessing that the same conversations were happening at the software company. I can imagine its staff telling their managers what jerks were on the training team. I'm sure it irritated them that we continually were interrupting their work, making it even more difficult to finish the system. To them, it was much more important to complete the software development than to build training, especially because the software was what they were being paid to deliver.

With his fine stash

of new band instruments all ready to share with his brothers, Speedy turned toward his house. A few sticks lay at his feet and, when he tossed them onto the roof, it tipped at a shaky angle.

"Well, I'll get plenty of ventilation," he thought. He'd pretty well convinced himself that the wolf was long gone, so he packed up his instruments and went to look for his brothers.

Dusk was falling as he clattered across the clearing. In the distance, he could just glimpse a figure struggling toward him, pulling a wagon.

"Demmy!" he shouted, and hurried ahead to help.

"Speedy, thank goodness you're here. I'm about to give out. Please give me a hand pulling these bricks into the clearing."

Speedy stared at the wagon and couldn't think of anything he'd less like to do. "Demmy," he pleaded, "forget this house business. I've found a way to make instruments out of sticks! We'll form a band and make so much money that we can pay the wolf off, if he ever comes back."

Demmy was furious. "Speedy, this is serious. The wolf's probably watching us from the woods right now, just waiting for a good time to strike! Haven't you built any house at all?"

"Well, sure I have," Speedy answered. "It's over there—the one made from sticks. Let's go there and get a good night's sleep, and we can talk more about this in the morning."

Demmy shook his head and tugged on the wagon pull. With a shrug, Speedy went looking for Goldy.

He found that brother struggling with the last touches on his unstable structure—and in a nasty mood, too.

"Are you crazy?" Goldy screamed, as Speedy tried to tell him about the band. "I've finally finished this stupid house, and I'm over it! Just leave me alone. I'm going to sleep." And he very carefully edged into his cardboard-topped cabin.

"Fiddle-dee-dee," thought Speedy, "It'll all be better tomorrow." Then he carried his sticks back across the clearing and went to bed.

This interpersonal dynamic is so common on projects! There's always an *us* and a *them*. Whether it's the project team and the business sponsors, or the IT developers and the subject-matter experts, people naturally build alliances to protect themselves from other alliances. Business has a long tradition of encouraging competing tribes on project teams. It's so easy to slip into this dynamic. Add increasing stress to the situation as the project progresses, and you can have outright civil war.

In his book *Selling the Dream,* Guy Kawasaki talks about the value to a team of having a strategic enemy. Nothing unites a group of people faster than a common foe. Unfortunately, teams left to their own devices often will pick a completely inappropriate enemy and thus damage the velocity of the project. Stakeholders who turn on each other challenge a project timeline more than anything else that can happen.

A project's success comes from delivering the right solution to a business challenge or opportunity. One stakeholder can't be successful at the expense of another. In a project that develops new software applications and puts that software successfully into use, how can the software be implemented effectively without good training? How can good training occur without good software? *Us* against *them* is common, but it's selfish and mutually destructive. It helps no one.

The project manager owns the *success or failure* of the project, and, thus, is responsible for keeping all the stakeholders connected in a positive way. Adversarial relationships aren't built suddenly—they develop. Collaboration is the same—it's a moment-by-moment, individual decision. Each day, in a thousand different conversations, you'll be faced with the subtle decision to choose conflict or collaboration, as will every stakeholder. Many times you'll really want to pick conflict. The smart project managers, however, know that the way to win is to seek first to collaborate, no matter what.

Collaboration doesn't mean that there will be no conflict. Conflict is a good thing on projects, ensuring that teams are learning from each other and moving in the same direction. (You'll learn more about conflict and negotiating in Step 8.)

STEP **5**

In this step, which is still part of the **Define** phase, you'll set the stage for practicing great project leadership. You'll state and communicate the vision of the project, coach and delegate effectively, treat each stakeholder in a way that is uniquely suitable, hold productive meetings, and practice being resilient in the face of change.

Time to Complete This Step

The act of collaborating takes only seconds at a time, but it must be practiced many times a day. The amount of time you'll spend leading is proportional to the project risk. Consider blocking time to think about collaboration at the same time each week. What things that have happened during the week have prompted feelings of anger? How has this anger been shutting down your communication? What can you do to build collaborative behavior instead?

Stakeholders

As project manager, try to get all the stakeholders and members of the project team together at the beginning of the project to talk about your project vision and how you will lead the project. Doing so will set a baseline for future discussions when conflict starts.

Questions to Ask

As leader of the project, answer the following:
1. How can I share my vision of the project with the stakeholders?
2. What leadership strengths and challenges do I bring to a project?
3. How can I delegate responsibilities and coach team members effectively?
4. How can I adapt my communication style to different team members so that I meet their unique needs?
5. How can I ensure that our project meetings are productive?

6. Knowing that the project will change frequently, how can I model and teach others the ability to recover from or adjust easily to change?

7. Have I said anything that might lead my staff to believe I support ongoing conflict?

8. Have I done anything that might lead my staff to believe I support ongoing conflict?

9. How can I help my team continually choose a problem-solving approach that promotes collaboration?

A leader must model the behavior he or she is asking of others. It's easy to get annoyed when the stakes are high and you're in charge, but the staff replicates the behavior of the leader, so you must stay mindful of how you're behaving all the time. When the leader screws up—and all leaders do—he or she quickly must fess up to the mistake and get behaviors back in synch with project success. Worksheet 5.1 is a brief assessment you can use to evaluate your strengths and challenges as a project leader.

The competencies that you rate as *high* are the behaviors you do well and are most comfortable doing. Other people most likely would describe your strengths in these terms. The competencies you rate as *low* are the behaviors that you struggle with. It's important to be aware of these, but it's highly unlikely that you could ever turn them into strengths. Instead, build a network of friends and staff who you can depend on to fill this gap for you. The competencies that you rate as *medium* can be vastly improved with a little learning (through training or mentoring) and practice. To validate the results of your self-assessment, you might want to ask a couple of your peers, your staff, and maybe your boss to tell you their opinions.

Project Manager's Toolkit: Create and Lead an Effective Team

As the project progresses, it becomes more and more of a challenge to continue to lead. In this section, you'll learn effective means of project leadership, including

- setting a project vision and getting others to buy into it
- delegating and coaching
- holding productive project meetings
- building resilience among team members.

WORKSHEET 5.1

Assessment of Your Project Leadership Abilities

Instructions: This assessment is intended to show you where your project leadership strengths lie and where you have room to improve. On each of the following abilities, honestly rate yourself *high, medium,* or *low.*

1. Build cohesive teams with shared purpose and high performance   RATING:

2. Set, communicate, and monitor milestones and objectives   RATING:

3. Gain and maintain buy-in from sponsors and customers   RATING:

4. Prioritize and allocate resources   RATING:

5. Manage multiple, potentially conflicting priorities   RATING:

6. Create and define systems and processes to translate vision into action   RATING:

7. Maintain an effective, interactive, and productive team culture   RATING:

8. Manage budget and project progress   RATING:

9. Gather and analyze appropriate input, and manage the "noise" of information overload   RATING:

10. Manage risk-versus-reward and return-on-investment equations   RATING:

11. Balance established standards with the need for exceptions in decision making   RATING:

12. Align decisions with business and organizational/team values   RATING:

13. Make timely decisions in alignment with customer and business pace   RATING:

Sources: Adapted from Lou Russell and Jeff Feldman, *IT Leadership Alchemy* (New York: Prentice Hall, 2003); and Lou Russell, *Leadership Training* (Alexandria, VA: ASTD Press, 2003).

STEP 5

Setting a Project Vision

For a long time, vision has been acknowledged as an essential quality of leadership. But vision is still something not entirely understood by everyone. Even when the trait is understood, the practice is rarely mastered. This section will address the dynamics of vision—how we understand it as a concept, how we create it, and how we apply it to inspire achievement in a fast-paced, challenging world.

Vision is a vividly imagined sense of a desired future. It's the destination we aim for, the outcome we want. Vision also is a path we travel in carrying out our project's purpose—not just a destiny, but the actual journey in pursuit of that destiny. Vision isn't an answer only in response to the questions, what do we want? or where are we going? It also answers the question, how do we get there? Although it may seem that knowledge of the destination must precede the choice of paths, that may not always be true. Certain destinations only become clear when the journey along a specific path has begun—thus the need to keep vision dynamic.

STEP 5

We might choose to think of vision as a story. There is great power in story as a medium for communicating a message. Story captures the imagination, conjures powerful images, and creates strong connections. Vision is the story we tell about our future, and as we tell and retell the story, it becomes familiar to us. We come to know how it unfolds and how it ends—and we become attached to that ending.

An engaging vision is a key deliverable for a project manager because it offers the following advantages:

- *It provides focus*—In a world full of opportunity and distraction, a clear vision enables all parties to remain focused on the commitments we are making to ourselves, our customers, and other organizational business units. Constant attention to the vision keeps us on course and allows correction when things change.
- *It provides inspiration*—The inspiration it offers is what makes vision such a vital component of leadership. Leaders harness human potential and human energy toward a desired end, inspiring performance by getting people excited about their roles in the project.
- *It provides hope*—As the demands for speed, results, and constant change grow ever stronger, it's easy to become frustrated and disillusioned. Vision provides a positive, forward-facing focus—a we-can-do-this" attitude.

The vision of a project remains steadfast, even in times of rapid change. In fact, the boundaries and guidelines framed by vision help us navigate such change successfully. The essence of vision remains constant, regardless of the pace of change.

Information gathered and generated by the following questions answered in Steps 1 through 4 of this book have set the stage for creating a vision for your project:

1. What is the ultimate outcome we want for this project?
2. What will each of us have to do in support of that outcome?
3. What is our timeframe?
4. How will we measure our success? Who will measure it?
5. What benchmarks will we set as a means of measuring our progress along the way?
6. What communication process will we use to keep all stakeholders aligned and informed of the vision as it unfolds?

Now it's time to write a vision statement. This is a simple process that can be done during a one-hour meeting. Here are the steps to follow:

1. Ask each sponsor, stakeholder, and team member to write his or her own description of the project's vision, using three verbs and one noun. Be sure to be ready with several examples to get them started—but don't make them examples that pertain to the current project.
2. Make a list of all the verbs and a list of all the nouns used in the statements. You can do this by collecting everyone's work or by asking participants to call out the words while you write them on a flipchart.
3. Discuss the differences among the verbs and among the nouns, and come to an agreement on which one noun and which three verbs are most suited to the group's vision of the project.
4. Write a concise and meaningful vision statement from these words.

Do your best to energize stakeholders in this visioning effort. The more you can get them involved in writing the vision statement, the easier it will be to enroll them in the vision itself.

Example 5.1 uses our blog project to illustrate this process. Notice the difference in the three initial vision statements. Each one reflects the narrow perception of an individual. The blog project will create a blog, and if it's successful it will streamline product sales and enable the customer to communicate more effectively back to the company.

As project team members share their "local" views, it will become clear that there is an engaging, bigger-picture view that will require all of them to work together. A good vision gives you a reason to look forward to going to work. No one jumps out of bed in the morning saying, "Yeah! I can just get by today!"

It's common during this exercise for people in the first round to focus only on the project deliverables for which they're responsible, like technology or a new product, or new/more customers. Sometimes those narrow-focus deliverables are a means to an end—technology and products are obvious examples. Remember the importance of the business objective—increase revenue, avoid costs, and

EXAMPLE 5.1

Creating the Blog Project Vision Statement

1. The project manager received these three vision statements from project stakeholders:

    * *The blog project will design, implement, and build a blog site.*
    * *The project will grow, enable, and streamline product sales.*
    * *Our project will initiate, demand, and respond to customer communication.*

2. The manager wrote the following lists on the whiteboard:

Verbs		Nouns
design	streamline	blog site
implement	initiate	product sales
build	demand	customer communication
grow	respond	
enable		

3. At the end of the discussion, the group agreed to the following vision statement for their project: *The blog project will initiate, enable, and respond to customer communication through a web blog site.*

improve service. The final vision focuses on customer communication, with the technology as an enabler. When you're writing your project vision, it's OK to break the one-noun rule to make the vision statement more clear, as long as you keep the main object of the sentence clear.

Enrolling Sponsors and Stakeholders in the Vision

If the sponsors participated in the vision exercise, that's wonderful. In most cases, there are stakeholders who either are not available or are too high up in the organization to have time for project team meetings. But that doesn't mean you just leave them out of the vision loop. Rather, once your visioning meeting has produced a vision statement that everyone attending the meeting has agreed to, it's time to communicate it to all the stakeholders (including those who didn't attend the meeting) to secure their buy-in.

TOOL 5.1

Questions to Help You Get Stakeholders to Buy Into the Vision

1. What does this audience most want to hear? How can the vision statement appeal to, address, or satisfy that desire?

2. If your vision is presented in story form, rather than as a declarative statement of intention, how clearly will this audience identify themselves as vital characters in it? How can their character roles be clarified further and brought to life more fully?

3. In which aspects of the vision statement will this audience find inspiration? How can you maximize the inspirational quality?

As you plan how you'll present the vision statement to people who haven't been involved in fashioning it, remember that knowing your audience means knowing what will inspire them, and using that knowledge to your advantage means packaging your message accordingly. Use the questions in tool 5.1 to prepare your presentation to your stakeholders.

Visions must be communicated early and often—once is not enough. A successful vision statement comes up in discussions about changes and challenges. You may inspire your stakeholders and get their commitment through your initial communication process, but carrying out the agreed vision can be a long and arduous endeavor, and initial enthusiasm will wane over time. Stakeholder commitment must be reasserted and reinforced repeatedly as the vision unfolds. You must nurture the connection your stakeholders have to the vision to remind them of the value of the work they do and to continue fueling their internal fires for that work. This is one of your key responsibilities as a project leader.

The mistake that's made often is to confuse a *vision* with the actual written statement. The vision is so much more than its description. It's never enough to email a vision to someone or give them a document with the vision typed on the cover. A vision demands special treatment and repetition. Think of how you can make the vision come alive. Here are some ideas:

- Have coffee cups or coffee cup tiles emblazoned with the vision, expressed either graphically or in words.
- Make posters expressing the vision and have the project team and stakeholders sign them. Post them everywhere there's a stakeholder.
- Have a 15-minute, one-on-one meeting with the sponsor so you can share the vision enthusiastically.
- Mention the vision in meetings. Use it in your language as you work through project challenges with team members. When you're making decisions together, ask others, "What should we choose if we want to honor our vision?"

Dealing with Diverse Personalities

When the vision has been stated, everyone needs to know what they're supposed to be doing. Prior to building a detailed project plan that spells out each stakeholder's specific output and the pertinent schedule (you'll do that in Step 6), it's important that you know how to delegate project tasks successfully and how to coach as the work gets under way to ensure it all stays on plan.

Building a collaborative project team involves working well with various personality types. Whether you're communicating with stakeholders or your project team, behavioral profiles help you understand how different people interact with one another and react to stress and conflict. They also provide insight on how to adapt to different communication preferences.

A warning is in order: All assessments are just models; in no way do they offer a complete picture of any unique individual. They never should be used to judge others or to limit someone's career opportunities. Instead, be careful to use them as one indicator of the most effective way to communicate with another person.

In this section, we'll look at one behavioral assessment—the DISC profiles—and at how you can use the understanding you gain from them to build a project team that works well. It's probably true that the human resources department at your company has other behavioral profiles available for your use as well.

In 1920, William Moulton Marston developed a theory to explain people's emotional responses to various stimuli. The current DISC assessments, offered by several companies, are based on his initial research. DISC is designed to help people explore personality and behavior types so they can better understand themselves and others.

In the DISC approach, each person's profile is based on the combination of the following four primary behavioral dimensions:

- **Dominance:** direct, driver, decisive—*D*s are strong-minded, aggressive, strong-willed people who enjoy challenges, action, and immediate results.
- **Influence:** social, optimistic, and outgoing—An *I* is a "people person" who prefers participating on teams, sharing ideas, and entertaining and energizing others. This person likes to gain consensus.
- **Steadiness:** stable, sympathetic, and cooperative—*S*s tend to be helpful team players. They prefer being behind the scenes, working in consistent and predictable ways. They don't like rapid change, and they don't like conflict. They're often good listeners.
- **Compliance:** concerned, cautious, and correct—*C*s usually plan ahead, constantly check for accuracy, and use systematic approaches.

Worksheet 5.2 offers a quick DISC self-assessment for you to try. It's a short-cut, nonscientific way to get people thinking about their traits and ways of behaving in the world.[1] As you read

---

[1] To enhance your understanding of this assessment, I strongly recommend that you license and use full DISC profiles that are available from a distributor (see the Resources section). Additional readings concerning these behaviors also are listed in that section. I suggest you try Julie Straw and Alison Brown Cerier's *The 4-Dimensional Manager: DISC Strategies for Managing Different People in the Best Ways* (San Francisco: Berrett-Koehler, 2002).

WORKSHEET 5.2

DISC Behavioral Self-Assessment

Instructions: Circle all the words that you think describe you. The words you've circled indicate your behavioral preferences.

C	D
Careful	Urgent
Objective, clear	Pioneering
Has high standards	Innovative
Good analyst	Driven
Detailed	Likes a challenge
Picky	Demanding
Aloof	Quick
Fearful	

S	I
Steady and sincere	Optimist
Patient	Motivator
Empathetic	Team player
Logical	Problem solver
Service-oriented	Emotionally needy
Apathetic under stress	Inattentive
Passive	Trusting
Resistant to change	Poor with details

through the words, circle any words that you think describe you. Circle as many or as few as you like. When you're done, tally the number of words/phrases you've circled under each letter, D, I, S, and C. Everyone has a different combination of these descriptors. The letters under which you circled the most and the second-most number of words or phrases probably are your preferred behaviors.

DISC assessments measure how you behave, and how others would describe your behavior. Each person on your team may manifest any of the behaviors mentioned and has a unique combination of all of them. Each of us has preferred behaviors that burn less energy and generate less personal stress. In other words, some behaviors are easy for us, some are more difficult. In the first part of the self-assessment in worksheet 5.2, users circle the words they believe best describe them. The words are arranged in four blocks: DISC. Let's talk about what each of those sections reveal. We'll work from the top-right quadrant and proceed clockwise.

A person with *D* behavior tries to complete tasks as quickly as possible. The two key words for *D* are *urgent* and *task*. A strong *D* competes against himself or herself every day to get more done and, at the end of a day, will wonder, did I check off more tasks today than ever before? Not being able to finish tasks causes stress for a *D*, and that shows up as anger at others. Someone with a lot of *D* gets angry when someone else is preventing him or her from completing tasks.

A person with *I* behavior will try to sway people as quickly as possible. The two key words for *I* are *urgent* and *people*. A strong *I* is looking to others to get the positive reinforcement that spells success and, at the end of a day, will ask, did I get more people to like me today than ever before? Not being special and liked by others causes stress for an *I*, which shows up as hurt behavior.

People with *S* behavior like things to stay on an even keel and prefers that everyone be happy. The two key words for *S* are *diligent* and *people*. A strong *S* is looking to others to learn whether he or she is successful at keeping everyone else fine. At the end of a day, this person will ask, did I make sure that everyone I know was OK today? Studies show that about 40 percent of the people working at your company manifest high *S* behaviors. Not being able to take care of others causes stress for an *S*, and that stress shows up as passive-aggressive collaboration behavior. Someone with a lot of *S* always smiles and nods positively at you, whether she or he agrees or not. She or he doesn't want to hurt your feelings.

A *C* likes to do tasks perfectly and doesn't like to be rushed. The two key words for *C* are *diligent* and *task*. At the end of a day, a strong *C* will ask, did I finish a task perfectly? If it wasn't possible to do the work perfectly, the *C*-behavior worker won't have finished it at the end of the day. Not being able to take whatever time is needed to produce perfect output causes this worker stress, which shows up as redirection. In other words, a *C* will create or point out a distraction that gets people involved elsewhere so she or he can finish the task undisturbed.

People classified in one of those four ways typically are found in predictable company roles or departments: *D*s are executives, leaders, CEOs; *I*s are trainers and salespeople; *S*s are managers, individual contributors; and *C*s are programmers, accountants, and engineers.

Conflict comes from the clash of different behavioral perspectives. Obviously, a strong *D* and a strong *S* are going to have trouble working together because their perspectives are so different. Similarly, an *I* and a *C* will have difficulties. In each case, there will be a natural instinct for conflict with the other. Ironically, if a *D* learns to work with an *S*, or an *I* with a *C*, they complement each other perfectly, filling in for one another's weaknesses with their own strengths. Thinking of the likely roles these behavioral types will occupy, a project manager won't be surprised to see the conflict inherent in relationships between engineers and salespeople or programmers and trainers. Similarly, a manager easily can describe how the changing whims of a CEO make him or her crazy.

People with similar profiles also often have difficulty getting along. Two strong *D*s with two different checklists can undermine a project quickly. Two strong *C*s with different views of perfection can cripple a project. Two *I*s or two *S*s will enjoy each other enormously, but they won't get much done without strong leadership.

As project leader, you have to help people understand that, as a team, they can fill in each others' gaps. As different behaviors begin to impede progress on a project, encourage the individuals to adapt to each other by helping them understand their conflicting perspectives. This is a coaching effort that requires you to approach each staff member from a perspective that's consistent with his or her strengths. In other words, don't tell a *D* to try to be nicer. Help the *D* understand how seeking collaboration with others will help him or her check off tasks more quickly. Tool 5.2 summarizes the

STEP 5

TOOL 5.2

Behavioral Differences Based on DISC Profiles

	Dominance	Influence	Steadiness	Compliance
Descriptors	Ambitious, forceful, decisive, direct, independent, challenging	Expressive, enthusiastic, friendly, persuasive, stimulating	Methodical, systematic, reliable, steady, relaxed, modest	Analytical, contemplative, conservative, exacting, careful, deliberative
Needs to . . .	Direct self and others, be challenged, compete and win, be direct, take risk	Interact, be liked, be involved, trust and be trusted, have fun	Serve, be loyal, be patient, relaxed, have long-term relationships, have closure	Be right, follow the book, strive for perfection, have proof and measurement
Basic Focus	TASK	PEOPLE	PEOPLE	TASK
Decision-Making Style	Quick, little data, comfortable with own opinion, prefers new and different, risky	Quick, little data, comfortable with instinct, shoots from the hip	Slow, methodical, requires data, time to process change	Slow, needs to be right, analytical—facts and detail, takes calculated risks, organized
When in conflict . . .	Confronts	Finds win/win	Tolerates	Avoids

continued on next page

Tool 5.2, continued

	Dominance	Influence	Steadiness	Compliance
Weaknesses	Impatient, oversteps authority, does not listen well, takes on too many tasks, lacks diplomacy	Disorganized, acts impulsively—heart over mind, trusts people indiscriminately, inattentive to detail, oversells	Possessiveness, resists change, difficulty establishing priorities, internalizes feelings, too hard on self	Too critical of others, hesitates to act, overanalyzes, internalizes feelings, hard on self
When under stress . . .	Gets angry with others	Gets hurt, depressed	Becomes passive-aggressive	Creates diversion
Value to the team	Results-oriented, self-starter, forward looking, challenge-oriented, competitive, challenges status quo	Motivates others, creative problem solving, team player, sense of humor, negotiates conflict	Dependable team worker, great listener, patient and empathetic, logical thinker, will finish started tasks, loyal, long-term relationships	Objective thinker, conscientious, maintains high standards, task-oriented, diplomatic, pays attention to details
When communicating with this style . . .	Be clear and to the point, stick to business, present facts logically, ask questions, provide facts and figures, provide a win/win opportunity	Allow time for relating and socializing, talk about people and their goals, ask for their opinion, focus on people	Don't rush into business, show sincere interest in them, be patient, don't be abrupt and rapid, look for hurt feelings, allow time to think	Be organized, be direct and specific, provide data and facts, allow them space, don't force a quick decision

four profiles and how each communicates most effectively. You and the members of your project team will find this information invaluable as you work together.

It's most important that you model adapted behavior yourself. Learn to adapt to the different project team members, and work to communicate with them in a way that is best suited to their communication and behavioral styles. Adapting is also useful when working with other stakeholders.

Delegating and Coaching

As you develop the project plan in Step 6, you'll begin to delegate work to different project team members and perhaps stakeholders. Most of the delegation will occur as soon as the project schedule (Step 6) is complete and shared, but tasks will come up along the way as well. Each person helping will need different amounts of support as she or he completes the assigned tasks. Some people need only to see their names on the plan with a description of a task. Others need more help.

As project manager, you are responsible for the project meeting its objectives. The larger the project, the more people doing the project tasks. Some of these tasks (and people) won't be able to start until someone else has completed his or her work. That's why it's so critical that a project manager be able to

- assign the tasks to the people who have the skills and knowledge to complete them
- articulate clearly to the person (or people) doing the task exactly what is expected for successful completion, and then track the progress of the task as it moves along to ensure that it's on time, within budget, and meeting the quality criteria
- coach the person (or people) performing the task if there are concerns or questions
- manage the successful hand-off to the person (or people) who'll perform the next task.

Those are the steps of *delegating*. Delegation is **not** doing all the tasks yourself, taking over a task from a person who's struggling, or micromanaging someone as he or she tries to complete a task. Delegation is getting the project done through a team of successful, aligned team members. Let's take a closer look at those steps.

Assign Tasks

Think about what it will take to do a task. Look at the people available to you and decide who is best qualified to do this task. Ensure that each person's responsibility is *specific, measurable, achievable, realistic,* and *clearly defines the time it will take.*

Articulate Expectations and Track Progress

Starting with a full understanding of the tasks to be done avoids a lot of misunderstandings down the road. Remember the SMART mnemonic we used to create project objectives in Step 3? Use it again when delegating tasks.

Coach Your Team Members

Good leadership also requires monitoring progress and coaching, both if there's a problem with task completion and if the task's been completed extremely well. Sometimes people mistakenly believe that coaching is only about problems, but truly effective coaching occurs when the coach gives both positive and constructive/corrective feedback.

Sometimes we overstep the scope of project- or work-related coaching and we venture into personal areas. Not only is that inappropriate in a work setting, but it also may be unethical because very few of us are qualified as therapists. Figure 5.1 illustrates four ways that coaches may try to interact with the people they coach—advising, counseling, teaching, and reflecting. The shaded areas—advising and counseling—are not within the scope of project coaching. Personal problems should be avoided or redirected to the appropriate human resources staff.

FIGURE 5.1

Four Ways of Coaching

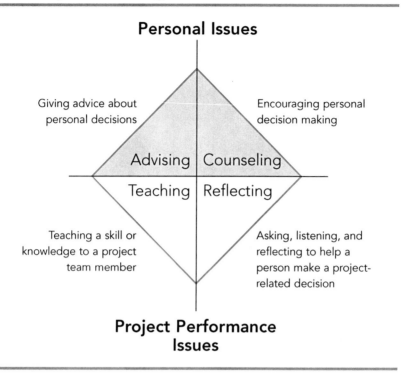

Personal Issues

Giving advice about
personal decisions

Encouraging personal
decision making

Advising | Counseling

Teaching | Reflecting

Teaching a skill or
knowledge to a project
team member

Asking, listening, and
reflecting to help a
person make a project-
related decision

**Project Performance
Issues**

Teaching means helping team members develop their skills or knowledge, either by sharing what you know or by lining them up with the resources they need to learn. *Coaching* means asking, listening, and then giving frequent feedback (both positive and developmental) on task performance. The coach is not "steering"—the coach is helping the person being coached decide how to steer for himself or herself. Coaching can take place in formal, one-on-one scheduled meetings or within small off-the-cuff conversations. The most effective coaching often happens in the moment, when you're talking in the hall about the project or someone walks into your office with a question.

The asking, listening, and feedback activities of coaching follow the four-step process illustrated in figure 5.2. For each person you coach, (1) assess what he or she needs; (2) together, develop a plan

FIGURE 5.2

Four-Step Coaching Model

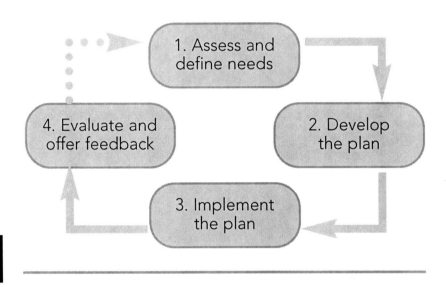

to make that happen; (3) implement the plan; and (4) evaluate the outcome as you provide feedback. When the person you're coaching moves away from the plan, your responsibility as coach is to start this cycle again. When the person is doing a great job, it's also your responsibility to provide positive coaching.

As a coach, you'll have times when you don't understand how a person could be so far off track. Before defaulting to conflict, consider asking yourself these four questions:

1. Does this person know what to do?
2. Does this person know why the task is important?
3. Does this person know how to do the task?
4. Has this person tried to do it?

These will help you avoid the temptation to make assumptions about what a person is thinking and what makes her or him unable to meet the needs of the project plan. Try to understand before telling someone else what to do and how to do it. Many project managers avoid coaching because they worry that they won't know what to say or that there'll be conflict. Good coaches know that coaching is more about *asking* than *telling*. Be prepared with a list of basic, open-ended questions to initiate a good discussion. Many times, good questions help a task manager discover how to proceed—and that's the best solution of all.

In addition, be certain that you clearly understand the problem or achievement and that you know what you'd like to happen—that is, what changed behavior would you like to see the task manager use to address the problem, or what behavior the task manager used that succeeded and that you'd like to support and encourage.

The following four questions will help you ensure that the information you're about to share in your coaching conversation is appropriate:

1. Is it factual—based on accurate data?
2. Is it free of emotion—calm, neutral, and not given in anger?
3. Is it fresh—pertinent to recent events or actions?
4. Does it recommend actions going forward?

If you can answer "yes" to all four questions, your feedback is ready to present.

Manage the Task Hand-off

When the person you've been coaching has completed the task, ensure its quality and begin the coaching process again with the next task to be done.

Holding Productive Project Meetings

On a recent television show, I saw a ton of tiny fish, minding their own business in their school formation, suddenly come under attack by sharks. These little fish instantly changed their formation into a spinning tornado. Although the sharks were able to crash into the formation and eat up some of the little fish, it became a much more difficult feat as the swirling fish confused their senses. If any of the little fish had broken out of the group, they would have been gobbled up instantly.

It would be nice if this worked for project teams under attack, and it's a strategy that's often used. But it always fails miserably. Let's say your project has just started. To be polite, and because you're still not really clear who needs to be involved in decision making, you have your first project meeting and invite everyone. People are friendly, exchange polite ideas, and most leave with a good feeling about this project. Then the trouble begins. Something happens that threatens the project deadlines or budget. Let's say the project is running much later than anticipated. You call an "all-hands" meeting for a number of poor reasons, including these:

◆ You don't want to deal directly with the people who are causing the delay. You think it's better to call a meeting for everyone and hope the remedial words land on the offenders. Maybe you don't even know who or what is causing the delay. You feel there's no time to figure out what the problem is!

◆ You want to get everyone involved in the trouble. This way, it becomes a shared problem and won't land on you.

◆ Instead of sitting down and figuring out who really needs to be at the meeting, you think it's easier to just email-invite the same people who attended the last meeting.

This dynamic creates a phenomenon dubbed a "Who Hunt" by some of my smart IT friends at Community Hospitals. Rather than spending time discussing a solution to whatever the problem is, the large group spends most of its time figuring out *whose fault it is* (certainly not theirs). If any solutions are tossed around, people leave with the delusion that change will occur—but no one leaves with a clear understanding of exactly who will own those changes. When more project deadlines are missed, you call another all-hands meeting—and again nothing is really resolved. Progress continues to decline.

Unlike the action that worked to save most of the little fish, schooling your entire project team in giant, tornado-like meetings doesn't keep the sharks away. Here's why:

1. Decisions and solutions can be created with greater innovation and speed when the only people who have both the authority and passion to create them are working

TOOL 5.3

Project Meeting Guidelines

* Identify the problem characteristics and hold a quick, informal cubicle meeting with the people who can help you get to the facts and who know how to solve the problem.

* If a person is slowing down a project because of performance problems, deal with it directly through effective coaching and performance-improvement goals.

* Grow your people. Give them the authority and responsibility to make decisions themselves and own their results. Be specific.

* When you're invited to a meeting, decline if you don't know what the meeting is about and how you can contribute. Defend your time.

together. In other words, get the people together who can solve the problem, but no one else. Less is more.

2. Giant project meetings are outrageously expensive. If you have 15 people in a project meeting for an hour, you have lost 15 hours of velocity on your project. Two days. This is pretty serious for a late project. Meetings are not free.

3. Giant project meetings are not a good communication vehicle. Problem-solving meetings when a project is late aren't good ways to communicate project status or goals or even to cross train. If the goal is to solve a problem, hold a meeting to do just that. If the goal is to communicate project status or goals, organize the meeting specifically for that or consider other media. Training is a specific goal as well. Don't use meetings to be all things to all people.

Use the guidelines in tool 5.3 to think about each meeting before you call it.

Communication

Good project leadership drives good project communication. Problems that challenge collaboration and breed conflict are going to occur repeatedly. I estimate that conflict adds 30 percent overhead to the work of each individual involved. Use the information in this step to help individuals work together to achieve the project vision by choosing to collaborate.

What If I Skip This Step?

Thinking about leadership isn't as easy as counting budget dollars, days, and heads. However, if you think honestly about what has made your past projects struggle, you know it always comes down to one factor—people. Leadership involves investing your time to get the people where they need to be.

What are the advantages of the practices you perform in this step? Here are a few:

◆ Setting a project vision as the groundwork for effective project leadership starts a project well. Effective delegation and coaching drive the likelihood of success.

◆ Using a DISC behavioral profile with your project team, whether at the beginning or during times of trouble, gives everyone a neutral language for explaining what he or she needs. It also helps people avoid conflict that comes from assuming certain behaviors are confrontational.

◆ Spending time planning and managing project meetings has been proved to be a leading predictor of project success. Letting project meetings degrade into Who Hunts will drag a project down quickly. The project manager is the only person who has the perspective and the authority to put pressure on project meeting participants to keep things collaborative.

Lurking Landmines

◆ *Stakeholders and key business experts don't have time to come to the meetings.* Approach them collaboratively and without blame. At the same time, be clear that the project deliverables can't be created without their involvement. Stress the impact on the schedule, without making it sound "or else." If key business experts really are unable to come to the meetings right now, the project probably should be postponed.

◆ *A project team member has a history of conflict with another member of the team.* At the start, talk about the conflict separately and honestly with each person involved and explain the behavior you expect from each of them. Carefully monitor the situation, and provide feedback for both good and less appropriate behaviors. If the two can't resolve their issues, consider removing one or both from the team. This type of conflict often spreads like cancer on a project team.

Step 5 Checklist

✓ As leader, model collaboration in all you do.
✓ Establish an effective vision for all the stakeholders.
✓ Identify the behavioral styles of the project team and stakeholders.
✓ Delegate and coach project activity successfully.
✓ Build a strategy for project meetings that increases collaboration through effective communication.

The Next Step

Next you will define the project in very specific terms. Now that you know the business case, the scope, and the risks and the constraints, and are primed to lead the project, you're ready to develop the detailed project plan. You'll figure out what tasks need to be done, in what order, and by whom to ensure the successful delivery of the project.

STEP 5

Gather Your Team and Make a Schedule

Work Breakdown
Structure

Critical Path Diagrams

Gantt Charts

Project Tracking
Spreadsheets

Now it's time to move into the **Plan** phase of project management. Here you'll leverage everything you know about the project and build a strategy to meet the business and project objectives. This strategy will include tasks, people who will work on the tasks, dependencies of the tasks, and a timeline. All of these factors appear in your *project schedule*.

In building a project schedule, you'll work with the following elements:

- **Tasks**—the specific jobs that need to be done to create the project output.
- **Milestones**—Points in the project where you stop and ask, How are we doing?
- **People**—the individual(s) best suited to each task to maximize the opportunities for success.
- **Dependencies**—the order in which tasks must be done to achieve success.
- **Time**—the hours, days, or weeks each specific task will take.

When Demmy

reached the spot where he planned to build his brick house, he dropped the handle of his brick-wagon. He was feeling a bit guilty about the way he'd treated Speedy. But, gracious sakes, his brother was always so quick to change course. Couldn't he see the real danger in BB Wolf? Demmy wondered how Goldy was faring but, if history was any indicator, he was probably asleep by now.

It was getting late. Demmy took a nervous glance at the wagonload of bricks. He had lots to do and not much time before deep nightfall. To organize himself, he took pencil and paper from his backpack and made a list of things to be done:

- get in the house and go to sleep
- stack bricks into a house shape
- unload bricks as close to the clearing as possible
- carry bricks the rest of the way to the clearing
- use the wagon as a roof, and put the remaining bricks on top to secure it
- check on Goldy
- apologize to Speedy.

Although sleep was his first thought, he knew it wasn't his first task. And he couldn't get distracted by his brothers if he hoped to get the very important building work done tonight.

"Well," he thought, "I'm the only one working here, so I'd better put all these tasks in order and estimate how long it'll take to do each one." He wrote up a new list:

- unload bricks close to the clearing—15 minutes
- carry bricks into the clearing—30 minutes
- stack bricks into a house shape—90 minutes
- use the wagon as a roof, and put the last of the bricks on top to secure it—30 minutes
- get into the house and go to sleep—5 minutes
- tomorrow, check on Goldy and apologize to Speedy.

By Demmy's calculations, it would be almost three hours before he could sleep safely, and with that goal in mind, he began his work.

In this step, you'll build a project schedule—a blueprint with the tasks, the people assigned to them, the order in which the tasks will be completed, delivery dates, and milestones. This schedule will be your guide for managing the project in the **Manage** phase.

Time to Complete This Step

The time it takes to build a project schedule depends entirely on the complexity of the project. It can take anywhere from half a day to a week, once the necessary project information is figured out. If you're going to load the schedule into project management software as well, double the time. Fight the tendency to fall into analysis paralysis. Build a "good enough" schedule because you'll be changing it. Perfection is not cost effective.

Stakeholders

Sharing the schedule with your stakeholders will help you in these two critical ways:

1. manage the stakeholders' expectations by helping them understand the amount of work that will be done
2. manage the stakeholders' commitment by helping them assign calendar time well in advance of the tasks for which they or their staff will be responsible.

Stakeholders may not care about the early project schedule details—just when it will be done. In fact, many of them think that

STEP **6**

how you get the project done has nothing to do with them, and that it's solely the responsibility of the project manager and team. The schedule will help stakeholders see the complexity of the entire project, not just the part that affects them. Your stakeholders may have strong opinions about what tasks need to be done, when, and by whom. If they don't look at the project schedule in the beginning, they'll likely find fault late in the project, thus creating disruption. As soon as practical, share with them the details of the project schedule, especially the tasks for which they're responsible.

Questions to Ask

Before you begin to brainstorm the tasks required to complete the project, take a moment to ask the stakeholders and the sponsor these questions:

- How many other projects will you be responsible for at the same time? Beyond your project responsibilities, what will your additional workload be? (*Explain to each stakeholder that the answers to these questions will help them understand how much time they'll be able to spend on the project tasks and how much additional help they'll need.*)
- Who chooses the people for the project team? Who is likely to be involved? What time commitments to other work does each person have? (*Explain to the stakeholders that this information will help them figure out how much time they'll get from other people working on the project tasks.*)
- Who will act as subject-matter experts on the project? What time conflicts do they have? If the subject-matter expert is already busy, it's likely to be difficult to schedule his or her time. If there are several experts, how will disagreements among stakeholders be negotiated, and by whom? (*It's not unusual for stakeholders from different parts of the business to have different views of the project requirements. This will alert you to dynamics that might stall your project.*)
- Are there any meetings, holidays, vacations, or other important time events (like performance reviews or end-of-year

processing) that will occur during your project? What impact will these events have on project work and on the availability of your project team members and stakeholders?

Ask experienced project managers and yourself the following questions:

◆ What has happened on similar projects in the past that unexpectedly altered the time required to complete tasks?

◆ What challenges have arisen in the past in working with these stakeholders, team members, and subject-matter experts?

Project Manager's Toolkit: Setting Tasks, Resources, and Schedules

A project schedule documents

◆ tasks to be done

◆ people who will do the tasks

◆ the task sequence—the dependency

◆ milestones, or dates for checking project progress.

These components are documented in different ways, depending on the size and complexity of the project. In most cases, you'll use

◆ a work breakdown structure (WBS) to identify the tasks required to complete a project

◆ the critical path method to illustrate your project's critical path network

◆ a Gantt chart to give a calendar view of the requisite tasks and a calendar view of those tasks by person

◆ a project tracking spreadsheet to chart projects that are less complex.

If you're using project management software, any of those documents can be printed once the project information is entered. In fact, you can enter the project task information by using a simple table or drawing any of the diagrams in the software itself. One database holds the project data and all the diagrams are printed from the same data. With a central database, whenever a change is made to one document or diagram, it's reflected automatically on the others.

If your project is not large enough to merit the use of project management software, you can create your documentary diagrams using drawing software like Visio or even PowerPoint. In that situation, of course, the project data will not be updated automatically across documents, so it's better to use fewer types of diagrams when you draw them manually. You'll learn more about each of these illustrative documents and what they're best used for later in this step.

The Tasks

Building a realistic project schedule requires some brainstorming. A work breakdown structure is the tool most commonly used to identify tasks that need to be done.

Work Breakdown Structure

Brainstorming using a work breakdown structure (WBS) is a hierarchy-illustration approach that helps you translate the big-picture goals of the project into the tasks (the work) that will be done to meet those goals. The WBS is not a project tracking document, and it isn't maintained for the life of the project. It's just a worksheet to get you ready to prepare your project schedule.

Let's look at example 6.1. It shows a simple work breakdown. A WBS resembles an organizational chart because it identifies and illustrates hierarchical relationships—in this case, among tasks. In the top box, usually called an "activity," you place the name of your project. At the next level down, you place a box for each big-picture sub-activity your project demands. The highest-level activities are arranged horizontally across the top; the lower-level activities break down into branches from there. (Although I've imagined that the project WBS diagrammed in example 6.1 has three big-picture sub-activities, I've only filled in the details of the first one—"Hold Project Status Meeting.")

When you've identified all the big-picture sub-activities, consider each of them separately. Is "Hold Project Status Meeting" an

EXAMPLE 6.1

Work Breakdown Schedule Basics

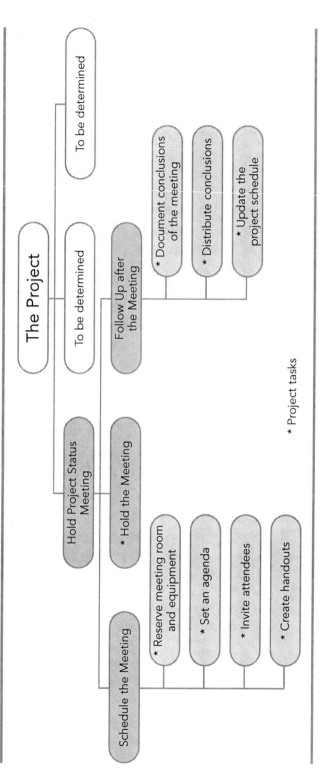

activity that cannot be broken into smaller tasks? Or does it comprise several lower-level endeavors? Although it might seem that holding a project status meeting is a basic task, there really are several actions involved in it. Identifying those lower-level tasks—all the way down to the most basic action—is what the WBS is all about. It breaks down the work of the project to its most elemental components—what we ultimately call "tasks."

So, what's involved in holding a project status meeting? Here's how I've broken it down in the example:

◆ schedule the meeting
◆ hold the meeting
◆ follow up after the meeting.

Next, consider each of those component activities to identify any lower-level tasks required. Are there smaller tasks to be done in scheduling the meeting? I think there are, and here's my list of tasks:

◆ reserve meeting room and equipment
◆ set the agenda
◆ invite attendees
◆ create handouts.

In our example, I've decided that "Hold the Meeting" is so basic that it has no lower-level required work. "Follow Up after the Meeting," however, is an activity that must be broken down to the next subordinate level of component tasks:

◆ document conclusions of the meeting
◆ distribute conclusions
◆ update the project schedule as needed.

At this breakdown depth, I think that the work is basic and measurable enough to be considered "tasks" and assigned to people.

To be clear here, "tasks" are always the lowest level of detail—the last branches on the WBS diagram. But the last branches don't always occur at the same level. In example 6.1, "Hold the Meeting" is a task because it has no lower-level work—it's at the end of its branch. However, activities at the same level as "Hold the Meeting" do have component tasks. "Schedule the Meeting" and "Follow Up after the Meeting" branch deeper into subordinate tasks, and it is those tasks that I'll put into my project schedule. Only tasks (not higher-level activities) are time scheduled and assigned to a person or group of people.

Even in our simple example, you probably thought of an activity that you would either remove, change, or add to my branch structure. That's the power of this visual exploration of what needs to be done—it's a way for a group of people to share their ideas and deepen their understanding of the project.

Here are some other points to remember about the WBS:

♦ Use your project's scope diagram to identify the highest-level activities. The data flows between the project and the stakeholders in the scope diagram point these out.

♦ An unlimited number of equal-importance ("peer") activities can be listed at any level of the breakdown. Your goal in creating this diagram is to bring to the surface every bit of work needed to accomplish the project.

♦ Any activity can have an unlimited number of component activities/tasks. If an activity has only one component task, it's not necessary to list it.

Tool 6.1 offers some additional ideas to spark your task breakdown brainstorming. Much of the research you've already done on your project will come in handy as you define project tasks.

A WBS can be quite extensive and complex when all the activities are carefully broken down, step by step, into basic tasks. In a brainstorming session, I find it useful to build these branching diagrams on flipcharts with sticky notes. Trying to build these charts with software is usually frustrating because printing all the branches on a standard sheet of paper is nearly impossible—unless you're willing to deal with type so tiny you need a magnifier. Because the WBS is a temporary worksheet, build it on flipcharts or a whiteboard, and take a digital picture of it for documentary purposes. WBS diagrams are not shared as part of the communications plan. Once the tasks are slotted into the project schedule, the WBS is no longer needed.

TOOL 6.1

Sources of Information to Use When Brainstorming Project Tasks

1. The scope context diagram:

   - Arrows going out to stakeholders show output to be delivered. What tasks will need to be done to get that output built?

   - Arrows coming into the project from the stakeholders show their input. What tasks will need to be done to request these inputs and to provide feedback on what else is needed?

2. Risk scenarios:

   - The risk scenarios you described earlier identified tasks needed to mitigate high risks. Have those tasks been added to your work breakdown?

3. Communication plans:

   - Each stakeholder requires some sort of communication from the project. What tasks will need to be done to ensure that each stakeholder has the needed communication?

   - How often will you hold project status meetings? Who will be there? What will have to be done to hold these meetings successfully?

4. Project management activity:

   - What tasks are you committed to planning, organizing, and controlling for the project?

   - What tasks are needed to measure the ongoing status of the project and achieve the milestones?

Your company may have a standard project method that includes a list of the tasks to be done. In training development, for example, there's an instructional systems design method called the ADDIE (Analysis, Design, Development, Implementation, and Evaluation) approach; and in information technology there are many system development life-cycle approaches, including structured, object-oriented, and agile methods. Standard methods are not meant to be applied in the same way to every project. Instead, they document the greatest number of tasks you would ever need. As an expert on your project, you'll choose which parts of the method are appropriate for your project. These preset methods, based on a good deal of research, are great ways to jump-start your project task discovery and they often prompt you to think of things you might not have considered on your own. If your organization doesn't have a standard method, search the web for some options. Many companies and public organizations publish their methods for others to use.

People approach the WBS in different ways. Some people don't like to brainstorm from the big picture to the detailed level—what's called "top-down" brainstorming. Some prefer to brainstorm only at the detailed level, and others start somewhere in the middle by defining the larger functions that need to be done and working down to the detailed tasks. Use whatever technique works best for you, as long as it results in a comprehensive list of the tasks needed to complete the project.

Task Assignments

Many project managers know how to build a schedule, working with tasks, dependencies, time, and milestones like pieces of a giant jigsaw puzzle. But the truly critical elements of a project schedule are the people assigned to the tasks. Everyone can think of a time when having the wrong person on a project team hindered progress.

Suppose you're ready to begin a highly charged, mission-critical project. What can you do when you're staring down the project gun barrel? How can you build a schedule that will minimize troubles and maximize success? At an address I gave on project management for the American Museum Association conference, I was approached by a woman who shared with me precisely those fears about a politically sensitive project. She asked for advice about what to demand from her stakeholders to ensure success. As she talked, she began answering her own question. "Sure," she said, "I know I have to ask for a lot of extra people since I can't ask for more time because we can't have it. The museum opening is fixed and advertised." When I told her I wouldn't ask for lots of extra people, she was surprised, and she pointed out that the nice thing about politically charged projects is that, at least in the beginning, the project manager has some clout to get more of what she needs. Here's why I disagreed with her approach.

Extra bodies don't help a project; they slow it down. If I were in her shoes, I'd ask for a few great people—quality trumping quantity. Better to have fewer people on a time-constrained project because the communication among them is more efficient. And it's vital that these people be A+ players. A highly political, time-constrained project is no place to develop talent.

In addition to being technically great, the people you choose must be superior collaborators. Great technical people with outsized egos will cripple a project like this. High-profile projects attract people who want to make a splash, get noticed, stand out. If the project is "all about me" for the people on the team, the team will struggle to work collaboratively toward project goals.

Your team members must also be customer centered, no matter what happens. Under stress, many strong and talented people become whiney blamers. It's rare to find people who can take the punches of a tough project, keep from pointing fingers, and continue asking the customer, What can we do to help with this situation? That doesn't mean that scope changes are ignored, but it does mean that the communication lines are kept wide open through a constant partnership with the sponsors of the project.

I've found that a project manager rarely gets to pick the members of the project team. More often, the executive sponsor picks a team for you to work with. When this occurs, make a special effort in the beginning to help your team understand how important it is that they be great collaborators and customer advocates.

If this truly is a mission-critical project, there's a decision that your sponsor can make that will be extremely helpful: she or he can dedicate each team member's full time to the project. Ask that the members of the team be gathered in a common space, away from the day-to-day crises and interruptions. The kind of single focus that an incubator-style environment will produce keeps the project on track and achieves the best results.

Research has shown multitasking to be counterproductive for most people, and the loss of focus expands exponentially when project pressures grow. Most of us do our best work focused on one issue at a time.

Task Estimating

With a compiled list of tasks and people assigned to your project, it's time to figure out the amount of time needed to complete each task. The word *duration* is used here to describe how long each task will take, but it's used in different ways as the project progresses:

Building the Best Team

- Start with a few great people instead of lots of mediocre people. Productive project teams comprise fewer people, not more.
- Don't pick people for their technical abilities only. Consider how they work with others as you make your choices.
- Pick people who understand the business and care about helping the business meet its strategy goals.
- Dedicate the team to the project as fully as you can. If you can't have team members full-time, figure out ways to have them work on your project in large chunks of time, rather than five minutes here and there.

- *Task duration* is how long a task will take a person with average skills working uninterrupted. The key words here are *average skills* and *uninterrupted*. This is the first step in estimating, and it's done during this **Plan** phase.

- *Planned task duration* is the amount of time you've set aside for a task, given the assigned worker's skill level and time available. The planned task duration is adjusted based on the person working on it, and this happens during the **Plan** activities as well.

- *Elapsed time duration* is how much time you think it will take for the assigned person to complete a task. This is the time on the clock or calendar that will be required to complete the task—this differs from *task duration* in that it presumes typical interruptions.

The differences among these three meanings of *duration* may be confusing at this point, so let's try to clarify them with an example. Given the task "reserve meeting room and equipment" from the brainstormed WBS in example 6.1, the project manager determines that an average-skilled worker doing the task without interruptions will need one hour. In other words, it will take the average person 60 minutes to figure out what person to call, to call him or her, and to give that person all the details needed to reserve the room and equipment. Therefore, the *task duration* is estimated at one hour.

Now let's say the project manager is going to do this task herself. She has scheduled meetings many times in the past, and she knows exactly which person to call and what to ask for. Because of her familiarity with the task, she'll use less time to complete it. She sets the *planned task duration* at 30 minutes. (Later in this step we'll talk more about how to adjust planned task duration according to the skills of the person working on the task.)

But neither the one-hour task duration nor the 30-minute planned task duration guarantees the actual clock or calendar time needed for the task. What if the person in charge of scheduling rooms is in an off-site meeting or away on family leave? What if there aren't any rooms available? What if the equipment is being serviced? So many uncontrollable things could happen, and they'll increase the time it takes to reserve the room and equipment. Our project manager realizes that some other work will interrupt this task and that there'll be phone tag or email tag adding time to it, so she takes all of that into account to estimate the *elapsed time duration*. This is the span of time, on the clock, that stretches from the moment she begins the task (decides who to contact) until she completes it (ends the phone call or email confirming the arrangements). She estimates that at four hours.

As you see, we have three amounts of time—one hour, 30 minutes, and four hours. Creating a project schedule based on the 30-minute planned task duration would severely underestimate the time needed to reserve the meeting room and equipment. In the real world, we rarely have time to work on tasks uninterrupted, and it's equally rare that everyone and everything we need to complete a task will be available at exactly the moment we need them. Therefore, it's not enough to estimate *task duration* or to rethink that estimate and produce an estimated *planned task duration* in light of the skills of the person doing the work. The real world demands that we go one step further and arrive at an estimate of the time a task will take when all the likely uncontrollable factors are accounted for—that is, the *elapsed time duration*.

It's important to note that all estimates of the time needed for a task are best-guesses. For making those guesses, experience and instinct are good foundations. The experience of people who've done these tasks before is your strongest asset when estimating the initial task duration. If you're new to project management, ask some of the more experienced managers you know to take a look at your estimates.

Most people are overly optimistic when estimating time. The problem is, of course, that you never work on a project task uninterrupted and no one has average skills. We've all been amazed when tasks of short duration took hours on the clock, and we've all been frustrated by people taking twice as long doing tasks at which we're expert. That's why the project schedule needs to show *elapsed time duration* rather than the *task duration* and *planned task duration* estimates that help you arrive at the actual clock/calendar time.

In Step 7 you'll be managing the project in progress, and you'll monitor a fourth time measurement—*actual task duration*. This is the amount of time the completed task really did take, and it's recorded during the **Manage** phase because it's useful for adjusting the project's ongoing schedule, and because it's helpful in learning lessons at the post-project review.

So, how do we convert *task duration* and *planned task duration* estimates to workable *elapsed time duration* estimates for the project schedule? In the early 1980s, AT&T Bell Labs developed an algorithm for doing that. Worksheet 6.1 presents the process for working from the initial task duration to elapsed time, based on the following factors:

1. The knowledge and skills of the person doing the task (termed the *resource*): Highly experienced resources can finish a task more quickly than the average person. Re-

WORKSHEET 6.1

Converting a Task Duration Estimate to an Elapsed Time Estimate

Instructions: Begin by writing the amount of time you believe the task would take a person with average skills working without interruption. Then follow the directions for making the three calculations.

Task duration: _____

Step A: Consider the Resource Factor: How knowledgeable about the business area and the required technical skills is the person who will be doing this task?

- ◆ With a highly experienced resource, multiply the task duration figure by a resource factor of 0.5.

- ◆ For an inexperienced resource, multiply the task duration figure by a resource factor of 4.0.

- ◆ For everyone else, make an assumption about their skill levels and multiply the task duration figure by a resource factor between 0.5 and 4.0 that corresponds to your assumption of their skills.

Step A calculation: Task duration x _____ = _____

Step B: Consider the Project Factor: How much project work really can be done in one day? What other project work will compete with the task for time? What is the project's risk level? How much extra time will be spent on replanning and communication because of the level of risk involved?

- ◆ If the resource will be dedicated to the task full time and the project has a low level of risk, add a project factor of 10 percent of the amount calculated in step A.

- ◆ If the resource is splitting time between several high-risk projects, add a project factor of 30 percent of the amount calculated in step A.

- ◆ For other availability and risk combinations, add a project factor between 10 and 30 percent of the amount calculated in step A.

Step B calculation: Amount calculated in step A + _____ = _____

Step C: Consider the Company Factor: How much time will be diverted from the project task by company processes and typical business tasks—taking vacations, holidays, and sick leave; answering email; attending training sessions and all-hands meetings? The corporate culture will determine to what extent this factor will affect the time needed to complete a task.

- ◆ Calculate 10 to 20 percent of the amount of time arrived at in step B, and then add that percentage to the time calculated in step B.

Step C calculation:

Amount calculated in step B + _____ = _____ **= Elapsed Time Duration** sources with little or no experience can take up to four times as long to finish a task. When you've factored in the abilities of the resource, you have moved from *task duration* to *planned task duration*.

2. The project's level of risk: Potential problems directly affect the amount of time that must be spent managing and communicating.

3. Interruptions related not to the project but to company practices and culture.

Example 6.2 uses the calculations described in worksheet 6.1 to arrive at an *elapsed time duration* for one task in our blog project. Notice that a task with a 20-hour *task duration* became almost 58 hours of *elapsed time*. Although this inflation seems stunning, we routinely underestimate how long it will take to finish a task. Did anything you did yesterday take longer than you expected? Enough said.

EXAMPLE 6.2

Blog Project: Conversion of Task Duration Estimate to Elapsed Time Estimate

Task: Create a high-level blueprint

Task duration: 20 hours

Step A calculation (assuming a resource with average skills and experience):

20 hours x 2 = 40 hours

Step B calculation (using a multiplier of 20 percent, assuming a project with midlevel risks and a resource who spends part of the time on the project):

40 hours + 8 hours = 48 hours

Step C calculation (using a multiplier of 20 percent, assuming an intense corporate culture that frequently interrupts project work):

48 hours + 9.6 hours = 57.6 hours

Elapsed time duration: 57.6 hours

Today's project management software can make some calculations for you because it lets you enter the percentage of a person's time you'll use. This feature is very helpful in large, interdisciplinary projects on which people serve as part-time resources, but it gets confusing when you're working with 10 percent of a person. For example, the program will tell you the person will be available to you four hours in one week, but how do you know which four hours it will be? The project management software considers only the resource factor—not project and company factors. You'll need to figure those out on your own.

Using the three-step conversion for every task your project requires would be too time consuming for most projects. As a short-cut, when you do your initial *task duration* estimate, think about the person who'll be doing the task and add the resource factor then. Then consider adding 20 percent for risk and 20 percent for company-mandated diversions. You can put dummy tasks into the schedule to hold this extension of time prior to each milestone. Or you might add one large task at the start of the project schedule to provide the extra time you may need as the project moves along. If you're using management software, lower the percentage of time each resource is available. That spreads the time required across the entire project.

Two psychological issues influence our task-estimating accuracy:

1. All of us estimate optimistically; we lean toward the best-case estimate rather than the most realistic one. In most cases, our estimates are too low.
2. If we adjust our estimates to make them more realistic, we know we've made that adjustment and we think of it as "extra" time. We may become less attentive to tasks that are running late.

The three steps of estimating described on worksheet 6.1 and illustrated in example 6.2 can help with the first psychological issue, but may encourage the second. Remember, you're not adding "extra" time; you're making the estimate realistic. To overcome any negative results of these psychological issues, approach estimating in the following way:

1. Build your initial *task duration* estimate based on your historical experience, and lean toward a reasonable rather than a best-case estimate.
2. Consider who will be working on the tasks, and inflate the task according to the guidelines in conversion step A.
3. Determine the best way to acknowledge that you will use an additional 10–20 percent of the project time for project management, and 10–20 percent of the time for company "interruptions."

Task Scheduling with the Critical Path Method

Now that you've estimated how long each individual task will take, figure out the order in which the tasks will be done. It's time to plug all the tasks together, using the critical path method to create what's called a *critical path diagram*. This diagram will enumerate each task and show how the tasks depend on each other. If tasks can be done at the same time along parallel paths, the diagram shows you which parallel path will take the most time—that is, which path is critical. The project manager needs to monitor most closely the critical (longest) path of tasks because the project will be late if any of the tasks on that path are late. You'll update your critical path diagram throughout the project, adjusting it as actual task durations or project changes affect the schedule.

Critical path diagrams can be constructed using sticky-notes, drawing packages like Microsoft Office Visio or SmartDraw, or more complex and rigorous project management software such as Microsoft Project or Primavera. Your choice should depend on the complexity of your project and on how many people will share the diagram. Clearly, using software to calculate (and recalculate) dates saves a lot of time on a large project. When first setting up a critical path diagram, it usually is helpful to do your initial thinking with sticky-notes and then enter the information into software, if you're using any.

At this point, you'll also want to determine what the milestones of the project will be. *Milestones* are points in the project where you stop and measure progress. By definition, milestones have no duration, so they're not tasks. They do, however, have dates associated with them. For example, in the "Hold Project Status Meeting" branch of the WBS illustrated in example 6.1, there were tasks under "Schedule the Meeting" and "Follow Up after the Meeting"; and "Hold the Meeting" was a task. Milestones might be set up in two places—after the "Schedule the Meeting" tasks and "Hold the Meeting" are completed, and then again after the "Follow Up after the Meeting" tasks. On the project schedule, milestones show up like tasks, but they have only a date, not a duration.

Figure 6.1 shows you the graphic elements of a critical path diagram. Notice that the tasks on this diagram are represented by squares; milestones are represented by round-corner rectangles. Arrows indicate the relationships among tasks.

There are two types of dependencies illustrated in the critical path diagram: task dependency and resource dependency. Task dependencies occur when one task must be finished before another task can begin. (For example, task 1 in figure 6.1 must be completed before task 3 can begin.) Resource dependencies occur when more than one task will be done by the same person. (In figure 6.1, to show you resource dependency, I've assigned task 1 and task 2 to the same person so the project manager decides which task should be done first and which should be done second.)

In figure 6.1, two milestones are set—one to start the project and one to make sure that the first phase of the project is complete. Notice there is an arrow leading out of milestone 2; it indicates that there is more to come in the project. Remember, a milestone has no duration; it's simply a date monitored by the project manager. All tasks leading up to a milestone must be completed be-

FIGURE 6.1

Critical Path Diagram

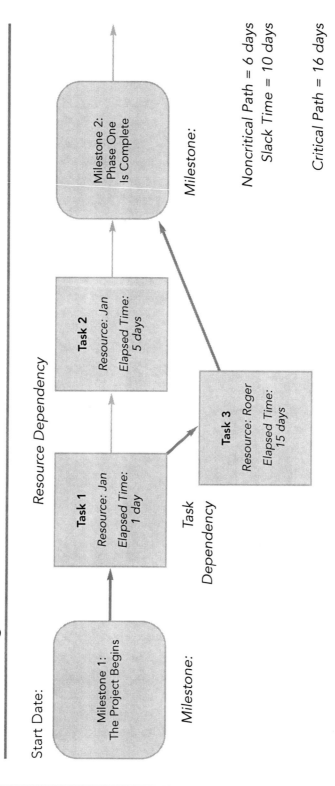

Start Date:

Milestone 1:
The Project Begins

Milestone:

Task 1

Resource: Jan
Elapsed Time:
1 day

Task
Dependency

Task 3

Resource: Roger
Elapsed Time:
15 days

Resource Dependency

Task 2

Resource: Jan
Elapsed Time:
5 days

Milestone 2:
Phase One
Is Complete

Milestone:

Noncritical Path = 6 days
Slack Time = 10 days

Critical Path = 16 days

STEP
6

fore the milestone date—and that's why paths that diverge along the way reconnect at the milestone.

The *critical* path is the task path that will take the longest to complete. Figure 6.1 shows two paths:

1. The path from milestone 1 (where the project begins) to task 1 (one day) to task 2 (five days) to milestone 2. That path duration equals six days.
2. The path from milestone 1 (where the project begins) to task 1 (one day) to task 3 (which cannot begin until task 1 is completed, and is estimated to take 15 days) to milestone 2. That path duration equals 16 days.

The path that includes task 3 is the longer path. Therefore, it is called the *critical path,* and the arrows indicating the relationships among tasks (dependencies) along that path are heavier.

The other path is a noncritical path. In fact, it's a full 10 days shorter than the critical path. Those 10 days are called "slack time" and the resources involved on this path have 10 "free days." The project manager can think about assigning some of the resources in this noncritical path to task 3 or to another project during this "free" time.

Project management software automatically calculates critical paths, slack time, and end dates (for milestones) on the basis of tasks, resources, and elapsed time estimates. In fact, if you're using project management software, it's best to let the software calculate as many dates as possible.

Now that you've seen what a critical path diagram looks like and how to read it, let's talk about how you create one for your project. Before you can build a critical path diagram for a specific project, you must have (1) a complete list of tasks and milestones, (2) a list of the resources assigned to the tasks, and (3) estimates of elapsed time duration for each task.

The first thing you do is to arrange all project tasks and milestones in order. This arranging does two important things: (1) it shows how tasks are related to one another, and (2) it begins to an-swer the question on all stakeholders' and team members' minds: When will my task(s) start and end? Your task sequencing depends on whether a task has to be completed before another (task de-pendency) or whether multiple tasks will be done by the same per-son (resource dependency). To do this arranging work, get some large flipchart paper and some sticky-notes. Get a copy of your WBS and, for each task, write the task description, the name of the per-son assigned to it, and the elapsed time duration estimate on its own sticky-note. Do the same for all of the project tasks identified in your WBS. *Remember,* only the tasks in the bottom-most branches are used for the project schedule. Arrange the sticky-notes in order on the flipchart paper, moving from a "START" milestone on the left to an "END" milestone on the right. Show dependencies by drawing arrows between tasks and milestones. For larger proj-ects, this may take several or many flipchart pages posted side by side on the wall.

In arranging the notes, remember these two things:

1. Tasks that are being done by the same person must be connected with an arrow to show dependency.
2. If one task must be completed before another can begin, those two tasks must be connected with an arrow to show dependency.

Tasks with no dependencies can be done in any order you feel is ap-propriate. Figure 6.2 shows how this sticky-note arrangement might look. In the process of putting these tasks together, it's not unusu-al to discover some new tasks or to decide that the brainstorming session broke some tasks down too low. The list of tasks taken from the WBS is just a guideline, not a hard-and-fast rule. Feel free to make adjustments as you create your critical path diagram.

Example 6.3 shows how the tasks for example 6.1, "Hold Project Status Meeting," would be mapped to a critical path diagram. Notice how the tasks that have been put in the diagram are the lowest-level tasks from the WBS. The diagram in example 6.3 is slightly more complex than the diagram presented in figure 6.1. There's a task dependency between "Reserve Meeting Room and Equipment"

FIGURE 6.2

Task Arrangement Using Flipchart Pages and Sticky-Notes

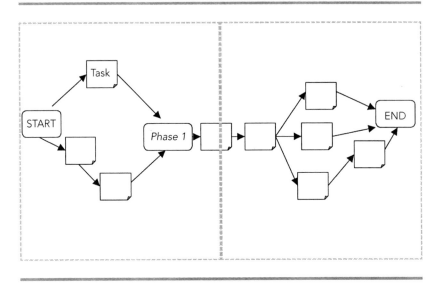

and "Invite Attendees" because you can't send invitations until you know in what room the meeting will be held. There's a resource dependency between "Set an Agenda" and "Create Handouts" because Roger is working on both tasks. You could make a case that there's a task dependency between these two tasks as well. These dependencies are shown by the arrows. The dark arrows show the critical path.

What would the duration of the critical path be for this diagram? Notice that the two paths leading into the task "Hold the Meeting" both have durations of six days. That means that both of these paths are the longest paths, so both also are critical paths. Moving to the next parallel paths that go out from "Hold the Meeting," the top path is three days and the bottom is two days, so the top path is the critical path. The total duration of the entire critical path shown in this example is 6 + 3 = 9 days. What is the slack time of the noncritical path? The slack time is one day because that path requires one day less than the parallel path above it in the picture.

EXAMPLE 6.3

Critical Path Diagram for Part of a Project

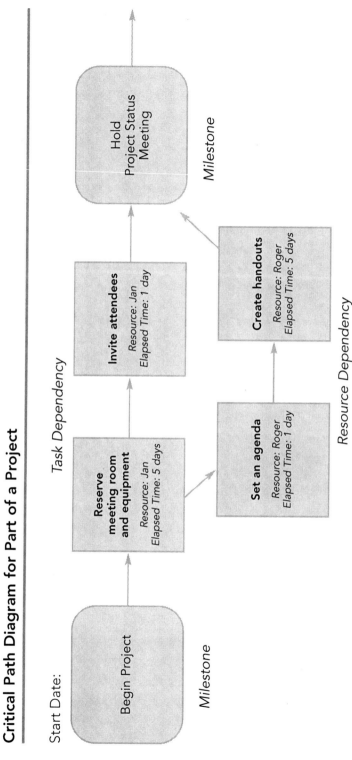

Start Date:

Begin Project

Milestone

Reserve meeting room and equipment
Resource: Jan
Elapsed Time: 5 days

Invite attendees
Resource: Jan
Elapsed Time: 1 day

Task Dependency

Set an agenda
Resource: Roger
Elapsed Time: 1 day

Create handouts
Resource: Roger
Elapsed Time: 5 days

Resource Dependency

Hold Project Status Meeting

Milestone

If you're using project management software to build your critical path diagram, remember that the slack time defined by the software is the slack time for the *entire path*—not for any one specific task. The software doesn't allocate the extra time across multiple tasks; and if one task on a path uses all the slack time, there is no slack time for other tasks along that path.

Task Scheduling with a Gantt Chart

A Gantt chart (named for American engineer Henry Gantt) shows the same tasks, resources, milestones, dates, and time estimates as does the critical path diagram, but it arranges them differently. Gantt charts depict progress in relation to time. For example,

- overall project progress across a calendar
- each person's progress in completing tasks across a calendar.

A critical path diagram is good to answer the questions, How is my critical path doing? and What tasks are dependent on others? A Gantt chart is good at answering the question, It's Monday, so where should my project be, what should my team be doing, and what's the status?" Critical path diagrams are useful for planning and adjusting schedules; and Gantt charts are good for managing project tasks and teams.

Take a look at the basic Gantt chart I've drawn (figure 6.3). It includes generic labels to show you what goes where and how to depict each element. This Gantt chart shows people down the vertical axis and dates across the horizontal axis. All the people involved start at the first milestone, indicated by a dark diamond. Notice that person 2 hasn't started any project tasks at the beginning, but the milestone is still shown. Similarly, all the people involved have ending milestones.

The length of the task bar depends on the amount of elapsed time each task would take. You can write the name of the task in the task bar or directly above it. Task 2, assigned to person 2, can't begin until task 1, assigned to person 1, is finished. that dependency isn't as obvious in the Gantt chart as it is in the arrow-defined critical path diagram. You can see that task 2 isn't scheduled to start until

FIGURE 6.3

Generic Gantt Chart

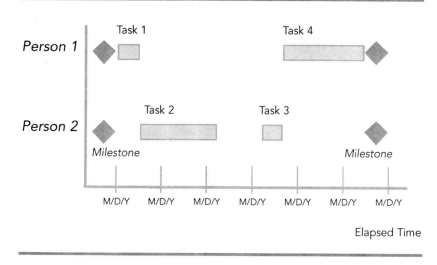

Person 1

Task 1

Task 4

Person 2

Task 2

Task 3

Milestone

Milestone

M/D/Y   M/D/Y   M/D/Y   M/D/Y   M/D/Y   M/D/Y   M/D/Y

Elapsed Time

after task 1 is finished if you look at the way the task bars line up, but you don't know if this is a task dependency or if person 2 simply couldn't start until then. Remember, information about task dependencies is easier to see on the critical path diagram.

Example 6.4 uses the Gantt chart to illustrate the "Hold Project Status Meeting" tasks we identified earlier. Jan, Jill, and Roger are working on this project. Notice that Roger's work begins at the Start milestone and he has some slack time to complete his last task before the final milestone. Jan begins work at the Start milestone and has slack time between her first and second tasks. Jill does not begin work at the Start milestone, and she has two periods of slack time between her first task and the final milestone. Using this view of the project schedule is likely to provoke some new questions and may help you uncover even more tasks. For example, why aren't Jill and Jan going to the meeting? How can Jill document the conclusions of the meeting if she isn't there?

If you use project management software, you'll find that different views of the project information can be created instantly. As

EXAMPLE 6.4

Gantt Chart for "Hold Project Status Meeting"

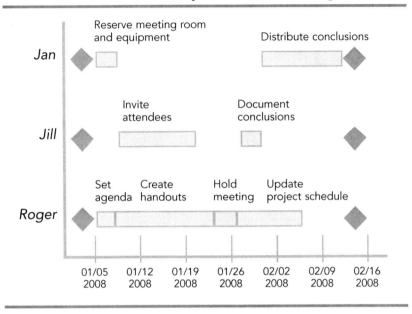

you learned earlier, the project schedule data are stored in one place, and the software lets you to look at them in many different ways: as a table, as a critical path diagram, and as multiple types of Gantt charts. It's difficult to draw and maintain changing critical path diagrams and Gantt charts by hand. If the size and risk of your project merit the time investment and learning curve, mechanizing your project schedule can be both a time saver and a tool to expand your comprehension of the project you're managing.

Task Scheduling with a Project Tracking Spreadsheet

If you have a small- to medium-size project, consider managing by dates rather than tasks. Use a project tracking spreadsheet instead of the critical path method.

Many of my projects are event related (training, facilitation, and so forth), so they're not as complex as some of your projects may be. To communicate with my stakeholders, I convert my critical path diagram into a simple spreadsheet (see example 6.5). Tasks, people assigned, and completion dates are included.

The critical path method works best when you're able to request a project completion date. The primary difference between my spreadsheet approach and a critical path approach is that I use the spreadsheet to manage to a *date,* that has been given to me, rather than to manage by task duration. In setting up the spreadsheet for an event to be held on a certain date, for example, I begin with that date (generally supplied by my sponsor) and work backward, subtracting a task's elapsed time duration to figure out what date the task must begin. As I set the dates, I keep in mind who's working on the tasks and all task dependencies that I've identified in my critical path diagram. Generally, there are fewer than 50 tasks on my list, so it's not difficult to keep all this in mind as I set dates. Example 6.6 shows how to start at the end and work backward to set the start dates for project tasks.

Notice in example 6.5 that I include both a project manager and a task manager on the spreadsheet. As is clear throughout these 10 steps, the project manager is accountable for making sure every project task is completed on time, within budget, and within quality specifications. But the project manager doesn't have to *do* all the tasks. The task manager is the person who'll be doing the task. In many of my projects, I wear both hats for some or all of the work, and I make that clear on the tracking spreadsheet. This spreadsheet helps me keep track of my project management responsibilities and my other deliverable tasks within the project. It also reminds me to check back with other people working on tasks on the project before they do get late.

The limitation of this spreadsheet is that it doesn't show task or resource dependencies. If you're managing a project that's too large to keep these dependencies clear in your head, a simple spreadsheet is not going to be adequate for planning or tracking. Select the critical path diagram and/or Gantt chart instead. But for any size project, a simple spreadsheet can be useful as a macroscopic communication tool to keep all parties informed. You'll learn more about this in Step 7.

EXAMPLE 6.5

Blog Project Tracking Spreadsheet

Project	Task	Project Manager	Task Manager	Helper	Due Date	Comments	Done
Customer blog	Interview sponsor	Jan	Jan		01/06/08		
Customer blog	Interview stakeholders	Jan	Jan		01/13/08		
Customer blog	Hold customer focus groups	Jan	Roger		02/15/08		
Customer blog	Milestone: requirements complete	Jan			02/15/08		

EXAMPLE 6.6

Working Backward from a Due Date to Identify a Start Date

Due Date	Task	Elapsed Time Duration	Start Date
2/15/08	Hold project status meeting	Milestone	—
02/10/08	Create handouts	5 days	02/05/08
02/08/08	Invite attendees	1 day	02/07/08
02/01/08	Set an agenda	1 day	01/31/08
01/10/08	Reserve meeting room and equipment	5 days	01/05/08

Communication

Having a project schedule gives you crucial data you'll track to monitor the status of the project, and it will provide information for you to pass along to your stakeholders. The schedule will change and, when it's adjusted, the stakeholders need to be notified so they see how the change affects the overall schedule. Their resources and tasks may be delayed. Remember flexible structure: at all times you have a schedule, and at all times you're ready to adapt it to meet the needs of the business.

Again, it's the stakeholders who'll judge the success of the project at the end. The more communication you establish in the beginning and maintain all the way through, the greater the likelihood they'll be happy when the project is complete. The project schedule is one of the most important communication tools.

What If I Skip This Step?

Don't. Doing the work needed to break a project down into requisite tasks, to arrange those tasks in the appropriate order with dependencies identified, and to plug all of that information into a manual or digital scheduling mechanism takes a lot of focus. But it will drive the success of your project. You can't manage what you don't understand. Even if you're the only one on the project, doing your work on the fly and dreaming up your next task as you go along absolutely guarantees rework, misunderstanding, and a last-minute crisis. That may explain the current statistic that 80 percent of projects fail to meet their preestablished goals for quality, cost, or timelines. Creating a good project schedule isn't hard; it just takes discipline.

Now, of course, the downside: Before you get your left brain too excited about this wonderful scheduling and tracking, be warned that the minute you finish your schedule, it will be wrong or obsolete. Something will happen to a resource or a time estimate or to the business and some part of your schedule will be upended. So it's good to think of the project schedule as an evolving blueprint rather than the Holy Grail. Keeping it up-to-date is part of the deal.

As fragile and mutable as the details of your schedule may seem at any moment, however, preparing a schedule offers such critical advantages (tool 6.2) that it's unlikely you'll be successful without one.

Lurking Landmines

♦ *You discover that you're not going to be given enough re-sources.* The time to talk about this is right at the start, not when your project is late. Don't be tempted to stretch the provided resources (most likely, *you*) by building over-time into the project before it starts. Planning "best case" is a dangerous and usually destructive activity. Talk about cutting scope or extending the deadline now.

♦ *The constraints seem to be changing.* Your sponsor told you back in Step 2 that quality was the primary goal for this project. Now, as you complete the project schedule, the sponsor asks you to get it done in half the time you've

TOOL 6.2

Advantages of the Project Schedule

* A detailed project schedule is your game plan. Everyone involved with the project—sponsors, stakeholders, team members—can look at the plan and figure out what's going on and, more important, what they're supposed to be doing at any given point.

* The impact of change can be illustrated and communicated visually through a well-maintained project schedule. When large change is brewing, the schedule will serve as a what-if simulator, indicating the downstream effects of a change at any point.

* The extensive detail in the schedule frees the project manager to work on influencing and troubleshooting. When everything is written down or charted, there's no need for the manager to explain every task to every person when it's time to perform the task. Kept up-to-date and used correctly, the schedule keeps the project manager from becoming the constraint of the project. If the only place project status exists is in the head of the project manager, she or he will be interrupted continually whenever there is a question.

* The schedule provides a detailed audit of what really happened on a project so people can learn from the experience and use those lessons on future projects.

planned. Not only does this alter your project schedule, but the constraints have also changed. Revisit the deliverables in Step 2 to make sure that you and the sponsor still agree on the **Define** phase deliverables, especially the business case.

Step 6 Checklist

✓ Identify the tasks needed to complete the project.

✓ Identify the people who will be working on the project.

✓ Assign resources to each task.

✓ Estimate the elapsed time duration for each task, adjusting when necessary.

✓ Sequence the tasks, based on task and resource dependencies.

✓ Set due dates for key milestones.

✓ Build a project schedule using the techniques that are best for your project.

✓ Send a copy of your project schedule to everyone involved.

The Next Step

The next step begins the **Manage** phase of project management. As the project begins, you'll learn to track your project status so that you see trouble coming early enough to adapt your project to counteract delays.

NOTES

Adjust Your Schedule

Once the project starts, the phone will ring. There will be news about the project that will seriously affect your project schedule. In this step, you'll learn how to adapt to these changes while minimizing stress.

Years ago, my company contracted with a large firm to create training on the processes required to run a new manufacturing facility. The decision had been made to build this facility, staff it, and open it in two months, no matter what. We were asked to propose enough resources to get the training developed in three weeks and delivered in two more. More than 100 people would be trained in 10 different types of jobs. The client agreed during the **Define** phase that the #1 constraint for this project was speed (time), the second priority was quality, and the third was cost. The sponsor was willing to pay whatever it took to get this facility up and operating in the time given. This was one of the largest projects we'd ever done, and we were excited about it.

The contract was signed but, surprisingly, it took a couple weeks. Our five-week project began later than we had hoped. The training course developers tried to contact the client to set up

STEP 7

Startled

and foggy-headed, Goldy patted the ground around him when his cell phone rang at midnight.

"Goldy?" said a quiet voice on the phone. "It's me, the BB. I heard that you and the boys were making houses to keep me out. I just wanted to give you an update on my plans."

Now Goldy was wide awake. And he knew exactly where he was—inside a box made of hay, cardboard, and trash scraps. He really never thought the wolf would come back, at least not so quickly.

"Uh, uh, that's mighty polite of you," he said. And he sat up so straight that his tipsy roof collapsed on his head.

"Well, I'm a polite kind of wolf," said the caller. "So, here's the thing. . . . I'm standing outside your house, I think—although the roof here just fell in, so maybe I'm not at the right place. Anyhow, I'm getting ready to huff and to puff. Then, I'm off to Speedy's to see what I can get done over there tonight. My stomach's starting to rumble, and ham sounds good."

Goldy hadn't squirmed more than five feet from the back side of his straw house before the hay was huffed and puffed away. He ran past the giant oak toward Speedy's house.

Speedy was sitting up, playing one tune and then another, when Goldy flew through the door. Some sticks broke away as he yanked it shut behind him.

"It's the wolf! It's the wolf!" he squealed. "He just blew down my house and he's coming this way. Are you sure these sticks will hold?" And a few more twigs fell out.

"Sure they'll hold," said Speedy. "You worry too much. Look, these sticks are sturdy enough to make beautiful musical instruments, so they sure can stand up to one raggedy wolf. Catch your breath and listen to my music for a minute."

Goldy didn't feel all that secure in his brother's house, but it looked much tighter and sturdier than what he had built. He guessed Speedy had spent a lot of time on it. Goldy'd been cheap—he hadn't had the money to build a place the way he wanted, and now he wished he'd worked with his brother instead of wasting time on his straw house. He felt like such a failure.

It wasn't long before the little pigs heard something not at all musical—a sound like a mighty wind. Little sticks, then big sticks began to fly around inside the house. The brothers, wide-eyed and frightened, crashed through the back wall just before it and all the other sides of the house blew across the clearing.

As they ran through the dark toward Demmy's house, the little pigs could hear BB whistling some music of his own.

In his neck of the clearing, Demmy was carefully securing his wagon-roof with the last of his bricks. He was exhausted, and it suddenly seemed he felt a chill in the air. Demmy slipped inside his cozy house and immediately fell sleep.

interviews with the firm's subject-matter experts and to get copies of the job processes to be taught. After many attempts to contact the subject-matter experts and the project manager failed, we finally got a return call a week later. Process documentation was sent to us, but it was neither complete nor final. The subject-matter experts were too busy to meet with our training people until three weeks later, and then the project manager would be on vacation the week the experts were available. It was starting to look like this was not a time-constrained project after all.

The constraints of the project obviously differed from those expressed by the client during the **Define** phase. If this truly was a time-constrained project, the firm's experts would be available to us and the project manager would not have been planning a vacation. The fact that the processes were incomplete and hadn't received final approval this late in the game was another warning sign. Although the opening date hadn't changed, every behavior we encountered suggested that time was *not* a priority.

As our course developers struggled to build materials without clearly knowing the client requirements, more conflicting clues emerged. The subject-matter experts reviewed our draft course materials and sent them back, saying that the topics needed to be taught in a different order or the underlying job process had changed again. Pilot courses were scheduled, but then cancelled. Two weeks before the facility was scheduled to open, we were notified that getting the new facility running was postponed indefinitely and the training would not be needed.

We were paid for most of the work that we did. When the contract was signed, I suspect the client may have thought that the facility might never open, but there'd been no official notification. Everyone acted with blinders, including us. Suspicious that changes were coming, we all found it easier to go forward with the plan, even though the plan made less sense every day. It was a great learning experience, but painful. It was nobody's fault—everyone tried to do the best they could with what they knew. Signs of serious trouble were all around us—and no one took a hard look. If we had, we'd have challenged the project manager and thereby avoided a lot of fruitless work on our part and a lot of wasted money on the client side.

In this step, you'll learn how to look for the signs of trouble and react appropriately before it's too late. We're now entering the **Manage** phase of project management, and in this step you'll learn the *zen of project management*. You'll learn to respect and listen to the little voice in your head that warns you about trouble before you see the actual proof.

In Step 4 you learned a couple of ways to gauge the risk of a project. Using the quick-and-dirty risk assessment, you rated the project risk based on project size, requirements stability, and technology. You learned that you can use the average of these three numbers to choose the amount of time you'll spend practicing the zen of project management.

You probably were asked to lead a project because you had shown real talent at completing projects. For example, gifted programmers who have shown an ability to deliver code on time ultimately will earn a chance to lead other programmers toward the same end. The downside is that the two different roles require very different skill sets, and "doing" aptitude is not the same as "managing" aptitude. When under stress, a project manager who's been great at "doing" will tend to go back to that same behavior to rescue the project instead of finding ways to engage the entire team. Project management is replaced by project doing—and the doing keeps the manager so busy that she or he no longer hears the inner voice pointing out warning signals.

Even if the project manager stays focused on managing, there's a lot to do: organizing and directing resources, controlling communication, and responding to revised requirements and other changes. A less active or less frantic practice, however, is frequently allocating time to think. Having this discipline forces the project manager to be more strategic about the project, looking at the future rather than just the problem of the moment. In Step 4 (tool 4.2) you learned how to determine how much project time you should invest in project management efforts based on the quick-and-dirty risk assessment. Now think about how much time you should set aside reg-

TOOL 7.1

Time Spent Monitoring, Contemplating, and Listening to Your Inner Voice—Zen Time

Quick-and-Dirty Overall Risk Score	Zen Time
1–2	15 minutes once a week
3–5	1 hour once a week
6–7	45 minutes twice a week
8–9	30 minutes on each Monday, Wednesday, and Friday
10	1 hour each morning, in company with the project sponsor

ularly for monitoring, contemplating, and listening to your inner voice—that is, how much time should be zen time. Tool 7.1 roughly estimates that time, based again on the project's risk level.

Notice that the greater the risk, the more time you must hold and protect to think about your project. And, of course, it's the higher-risk projects that leave you no extra time, so it will be extremely difficult to practice this contemplative discipline. No matter how difficult it is, I promise you it's the best insurance against project failure that you can get.

I've found it easier to dedicate a specific time each week to thinking about all my projects. I use Friday mornings as often as possible to review each project, update the project spreadsheets, and send status reports to my stakeholders.

Time to Complete This Step

Step 7 is about monitoring your project from the time the first task in the project schedule begins until the sponsor says the project is officially complete. The time you, as project manager, will spend on this step is proportional to the risk of the project. The higher the risk, the more time you'll want to reserve for listening to your instincts and taking corrective action.

Stakeholders

The stakeholders possess the clues to the real, current state of the business need that the project is funded to serve. The closer you stay to your stakeholders, the clearer the true environment will be. The stronger the trust, the more you and your stakeholders will be able to manage uncertainty with honesty, even though neither of you will *want* to face reality. The trust you established during the **Define** and **Plan** phases (Steps 1 through 6) will help you do a great job working through the **Manage** phase. Here are two ways that good project monitoring improves your relationships with your stakeholders:

1. Keeping close track of the project and regularly communicating project status helps you manage stakeholders' expectations by letting them know what you're working on, what you need to get it done, and how it contributes to the success of the project.

2. Checking in with stakeholders occasionally as they complete project tasks to see how you can help builds their trust in you. It encourages them and helps you earn their respect.

It's critical to remember once again who *owns* the project. The sponsor, who is funding the project, owns the business decisions and the project. All changes to the business objectives, scope, project objectives, and constraints must be approved by the project sponsors. You, as project manager, prompt and facilitate the discussions needed to determine and support these changes when challenges come up because you're often the first person to notice that things are not going as planned. It's the sponsor, though—not the project manager—who has the final decisions to make. For example, if you figure out that, because of new requirements, the project is

TOOL 7.2

Questions to Ask Yourself at This Stage of the Project

1. What is the status of the project? Which tasks have struggled? Why? Which tasks have been completed with no problems? Why?

2. What are the critical deliverables that are holding up progress on the project? Who owns them? Why are they delayed?

3. What decisions made during the past seven days concern you, even just a little? What is it about the decisions that have triggered this concern?

4. What did you overhear through informal channels that rang warning bells for you?

5. Who haven't you talked to in a long time? Why have they gone silent?

going to need either to be delivered two months later or to be reduced in scope, you would share your recommendation with the project sponsor, but he or she would ultimately choose.

Questions to Ask

The *zen of project management* is a term I use to describe the power of contemplation that all good project managers use. Based on your history with projects, you know a warning sign when you see it. Unfortunately, we often are too busy to listen to that inner voice and to adjust accordingly. To make time to correct this, at least once a week find a quiet place where you can sit down with the project schedule and answer the questions in tool 7.2.

When you give yourself time to focus, you let your inner voice move to a conscious level. In our hurried multitasking, it's normal to push the nagging inner voice away. There's certainly no time for bad news! But, as one of our customers likes to say, "Bad news early is good news." Most executive sponsors don't like bad news about their projects, but they'd rather hear it while they can still do something about it. As project manager, the earlier you can react to a change, the more options you have available to you for moving forward successfully.

Project Manager's Toolkit: Monitoring and Managing

In this section you'll learn techniques for figuring out when it's time to adjust your project definition and schedule. Many projects flounder because changes aren't made to the project schedule, rendering it unusable. It's important to note that if the business objectives, project objectives, scope, risk, or constraints change, the project definition will have to change as well. Once the impact of the change is understood, you'll apply a thought process you'll learn in this step to analyze your choices for moving forward.

Using the Project Schedule to Track the Project

In Step 6 you learned how to create critical path and Gantt diagrams to create a project schedule. At the outset, these diagrams show your best guess on how the project will go—and, in truth, the project *never* will go exactly that way. Once the first task begins, you use these diagrams to give you a visual model to monitor the status of the project. The critical path diagram is useful for adjusting your task dependencies and seeing how the changes affect the critical path, which predicts the project's completion date. The Gantt diagram can show you how the elapsed time on the clock or calendar will be affected by changes, including the scheduling of people working on the tasks.

Although it's tempting, when you're pressed for time, to skip the updates or just throw some additional tasks on it without really thinking of their effect, that's a temptation you must avoid. A well-maintained schedule is absolutely necessary. Updating your critical path diagram, your Gantt chart, or even your tracking spreadsheet (on smaller projects) shows you the downstream effects of upstream changes. Use the questions in tool 7.3 when you're changing the project schedule to ensure that the change hasn't messed up something else.

If you're using project management software on larger projects, you'll be able to enter *actual* task duration while keeping the

TOOL 7.3

Questions to Ask When Revising the Schedule Diagrams

1. Which tasks depend on others, and thus can't be started any earlier?
2. Which tasks depend on the same resources, and thus can't be done at the same time?
3. Which stakeholders will be most affected by these changes?
4. How will I communicate quickly and effectively with the affected stakeholders?
5. What will be the impact on the milestones (dates)?
6. What will be the impact on the people working on the project? As the tasks are pushed farther out on the calendar, will key resources still be available?

planned task duration for historical purposes. The software will let you visit your planned view and your actual view at the end of the project so you can learn from the gap.

As mentioned in Step 6, adding actual duration to tasks can change the tasks that are on the critical path and the slack time for other paths. The software recalculates the dates based on the actual task duration as soon as that's entered. It's not unusual for a delayed task to cause the critical path to change. In other words, the path on which a delayed task is positioned has now become the longest path—and that makes it the critical path.

Information Updating Options

It requires discipline and time to keep the project schedule up-to-date with project management software. To collect and update actual task durations on a large project can be a full-time job. It's a good idea to have someone play the role of project librarian or administrator, responsible for keeping all the documentation current and for handling status communications. If your project isn't large enough to need this kind of detail, consider using the spreadsheet approach.

Maintaining the critical path diagram as changes occur will help you keep a steady focus on the most critical tasks. A good project manager knows to keep one eye on the critical path while monitoring the other paths—at any moment, the path that is critical may change.

Emailing the Tracking Spreadsheet

You learned about the project tracking spreadsheet in Step 6. On small to medium-size projects, the critical path diagram may not be as important to maintain, and the tracking spreadsheet may be enough. When there are fewer people working on the project, there are fewer parallel task paths to monitor. The project tracking spreadsheet manages the project from a due-date perspective rather than a task-completion perspective. In other words, a row in the spreadsheet may show you that the task has to be done by the first of next month; the duration is really irrelevant.

The tracking spreadsheet is a vital tool for managing expectations with your stakeholders. As tasks are completed, you'll update this spreadsheet each week. From the start of the project, send the updated version of the spreadsheet to your stakeholders on a regular basis, ideally at the same time each week. Create a pattern of regular communication. Example 7.1 is a sample email that includes a current spreadsheet in the body of the email.

When you update your spreadsheet, color-code the rows and include the explanatory legend in each email. I like to use red for late tasks, blue for tasks that are in progress, strikethroughs for tasks that we've agreed to delete from the plan, and black for tasks

Tips for the Project Spreadsheet

When using a spreadsheet to monitor the plan, and managing to a due date rather than a task, it's very easy to overestimate how much work can be done by a specific date. Keep an eye on your resources, especially those who are working on other things at the same time. Whenever possible, under-promise and over-deliver.

EXAMPLE 7.1

Sample Project Update Email

From: Lou Russell [mailto:lou@russellmartin.com]

Sent: Friday, April 21, 2007 11:30 AM

To: M.Y. Customer, mycustomer@lol.com

Subject: Project Schedule Update

Here is the project schedule for the May class beginning 5/22 in preparation for our call tomorrow at 10 AM. I have sorted all the completed tasks to the top so we don't have to worry about them ('X' in the far-right column). Here are the things to resolve tomorrow:

- Discuss feedback from Mark and finalize agenda, development work to be done
- Strategize and focus on the development of the script from Desiderata (I think this is the #1 priority at this time)
- Finalize the statement of work.

I will call Beth's number unless I hear otherwise. Thanks!

Lou Russell

President
Russell Martin & Associates
(317) 475-9311
www.russellmartin.com

FUN, FAST, FLEXIBLE, MEASURABLE LEARNING

STEP
7

continued on next page

STEP
7

Legend: BLACK = pending; STRIKETHROUGH = not being done; BLUE = in progress; RED = late

Project	Task	Project Manager	Task Manager	Helper	Due Date	Comments	Done
LeadMay07	Reserve dates for class	Lou	Margie	Margie	2/6/07		X
LeadMay07	Write statement of work	Lou	Vija	Vija	2/8/07	Draft to Beth	X
~~LeadMay07~~	~~Conduct learning audit~~	~~Lou~~	~~Lou~~	~~Lou~~	~~2/20/07~~	No learning audit (customer did its own)	X
LeadMay07	Assign project manager	Lou	Lou	Lou	2/27/07		X
LeadMay07	Assign course developer	Lou	Lou	Lou	2/27/07		X
LeadMay07	Reserve facilitators	Lou	Margie	Margie	2/27/07	Lou, Susan, Mary	
LeadMay07	Reserve coaches	Lou	Margie	Margie	2/27/07	Deb, Karl, and Mike D.	
~~LeadMay07~~	~~Modify 360~~	~~Lou~~	~~Lou~~	~~Lou~~	~~2/27/07~~	No modifications	
LeadMay07	Make project schedule	Lou	Lou	Lou	3/23/07		

LeadMay07	Straw dog—agenda	Lou	Lou	Lou	3/23/07	
LeadMay07	Set learning objectives	Lou	Lou	Lou	3/23/07	
LeadMay07	Talk with Mark	Lou	Ann	Beth	3/23/07	
LeadMay07	Start holding speakers	Lou	Ann	Beth	3/23/07	
LeadMay07	Have 360 approved by customer	Lou	Margie	Lou	4/17/07	
LeadMay07	Send "Will hear from RMA" email	Lou	Margie	Lou	4/17/07	
~~LeadMay07~~	~~Input modified 360 questions to software~~	~~Lou~~	~~Margie~~	~~Margie~~	~~4/17/07~~	No modifications

163

that are pending. Color adds a level of instant comprehension when the legend is understood. I indicate completed items with an "X" in the *Done* column so they can be sorted to the top. Including the completed tasks is important to show progress so everyone feels part of the success.

Managing Issues When They Arise

In Step 4 you learned to identify, analyze, and plan for risk. Once a project starts, issues arise. The difference between a *risk* and an *issue* is that a risk is an anticipated possibility, but an issue really has happened. Some issue will affect a task, the project schedule, and/or the budget. You'll need to identify and address the issue in a creative way, and that will minimally affect the project's forward progress.

When an issue arises, your first instinct as manager is to react quickly—to jump to solving the problem immediately. Reacting quickly to an issue without thinking about all of the ramifications can cause more problems than the issue itself. It's better to use the guidelines in tool 7.4 and think through the issue in detail before you move forward.

Checking the Warning Signs

There are very clear warning signs when a project's priorities are changing. Tool 7.5 has a complete list of questions you can ask yourself to help you see these signs, and below we'll look at the signs in detail.

Warning Sign 1: Faces Are Missing

Not seeing your project sponsors face to face or not communicating with them in some two-way fashion over more than a week is one of the most telling signs of trouble. If your project sponsors don't hear from you on a regular basis, they'll assume the worst. You may feel relieved if you don't hear from your project sponsor regularly, but you also may be losing your sponsor to a new job or a new

TOOL 7.4

Guidelines for Dealing with Issues

* Analyze the problem causing the issue. Move past the symptoms to the real causes. Don't jump to a solution before you understand the issue.

* Determine the impact on the project. Which of these elements does the issue affect: business objectives, project objectives, scope, risk, constraints, resources, schedule, budget, or some other aspect?

* Decide who owns the issue so you can identify who needs to be involved in the solution. Make the following determinations:

    * Who has the decision-making authority to act on the issue?

    * Does this person know the decision belongs to her or him?

    * When should the issue be brought to higher-level attention (escalated)?

    * Is moving the issue up the line a positive thing?

    * Is the escalation path clearly defined?

* Identify potential solutions when escalating an issue.

* Involve project sponsors when needed.

---

company. If face-to-face interactions are too difficult to schedule, a less personal form of communication (like email) in both directions must be regular and predictable in its timing.

As part of your communication plan, make sure that high-level and factual project status reports are getting to your sponsor(s) each week.

Warning Sign 2: Status Meetings Become "Who Hunts"

You're getting a leading indicator that it's time to step into team dynamics when project status meetings become Who Hunts—ineffective gatherings where time is spent trying to blame someone instead of moving forward to a solution.

When your status meetings are eaten up by ineffective blame games, you have a team that's confused about direction and roles.

TOOL 7.5

Questions to Ask When You Go Looking for Trouble

1. How often are you meeting with sponsors? (warning sign #1)
2. How effective are your project status meetings? (warning sign #2)
3. How accurate have the task estimates been so far? (warning sign #3)
4. Are there key sponsors who may be leaving? (warning sign #4)
5. How often does the core project team meet? (warning sign #5)
6. Are the team and stakeholders still engaged? (warning sign #6)
7. Are there new project risk factors being discovered? When was the last risk assessment performed? (warning sign #7)
8. Has the scope of the project changed? (warning sign #8)
9. Are any key stakeholders leaving the project? (warning sign #9)
10. How healthy are the team members? (warning sign #10)

Additional questions to think about include

- Is the project documentation up-to-date?
- Are there regular communications with all the stakeholders?
- What are your instincts telling you about the current state of the project?

Lead people through a discussion about the problems they have. Let people express themselves honestly, then help them work through the conflict so they can perform effectively again. An effective project meeting drives project success. Ineffective meetings burn project hours with no benefit.

Warning Sign 3: An Early Task Is Greatly Underestimated

If one of the early tasks on your project schedule takes several times as long as you had estimated, there are two ways you can view the delay. You can write it off as an understandable ramping-up fluke and just resolve to make up the time on later tasks, or you can consider this a serious sign of ultimate danger and make massive changes to your project schedule.

Email Tip

Including the spreadsheet in the body of the email rather than as an attached file keeps the stakeholders from doing their own updating and sending their version of the spreadsheet back to you. If every stakeholder can make alterations, you'll chew up a lot of valuable time trying to get the different views back together. If you cut and paste the spreadsheet into the body of the email, people will be forced to send you an email update explaining their changes. This lets you compile all the requested revisions and resolve conflicting changes from multiple stakeholders. If, instead, everyone updated the same spreadsheet and sent it back to you, some changes surely would be lost.

If the obvious choice to you is to catch up later, know this: *that choice is insane.* A task coming in late at the beginning is the leading edge of a trend, not a fluke. The right choice is to look at the project schedule and figure out what you'd do if *all* the tasks took three times as long as you've estimated. *Gulp.* Take this sign as a gift and adjust your schedule now, before it's too late.

Warning Sign 4: Email Recipients Change

Keep an eye on formal emails. When you start noticing changes in who is copied on project emails, red lights should go on all around you. On one of my recent projects I noticed that suddenly my project sponsors were no longer copying the company president on project status documentation. He left the company shortly thereafter.

Warning Sign 5: There Is No Time for Status Meetings

It's a signal if you get too busy with other duties to hold a status meeting or people stop showing up for meetings. There could be several causes. Maybe people on the team believe they're fully aligned and don't need to spend time talking. This is a great feeling of a healthy team, but can create a surprising negative side effect. Any team that doesn't talk eventually will find itself misaligned. When things are going well, keep the meetings brief and to the point. Standing appointments work well for early meetings.

It's also possible that the project is starting to tank and everyone's afraid to talk about it. Of course, this is the exact time when a project status meeting is critical. Do whatever you must to get the right people in the meetings.

A third possibility is that the meetings have become tedious. The same people speak, and the same topics are covered over and over again. Get some help from your HR organization or local consultants to make your meetings productive again—create some new facilitation techniques, help people listen more effectively, and design more effective ways to resolve and track issues. Sometimes a little change is all participants need to be attentive again.

Warning Sign 6: The Silence Is Deafening

It's a bad sign when you stop hearing from people. Track how many project-related emails you get every day. This number should never go down—only up. Email quantity decreasing might indicate that the project is no longer a business priority and is about to be cancelled.

Warning Sign 7: Risk Factors Appear to Have Changed

If you're taking advantage of your contemplative zen time, your inner voice will tell you when a new risk appears. Be aware of what you observe and hear all around you, and let your intuition speak. If you believe something is posing an unanticipated risk to the success of the project, bring it up at a private or group meeting with your sponsors or stakeholders. Don't ignore it until it's too late to mitigate.

Warning Sign 8: Scope Has Changed

If one of the subject-matter experts or sponsors says to you, "It's only a little change; thanks for doing me this favor," and you make the change, you're in trouble. A task cloaked as a favor can kill your project because it sets a dangerous precedent that it's OK to ignore the project schedule and expand the scope. Be vigilant and help your team be vigilant against sneak attacks. Scope change must be handled the same way each time. Everyone has to know it's there and agree to it, and then resources have to be adjusted accordingly.

Warning Sign 9: Some Team Member Is Really Dressed Up

There's an interview in that person's immediate future. It doesn't have to be the sponsor to have serious repercussions on the project. It can be any critical member of your project team. Talk privately with this person to see what you can do to keep her or him.

Warning Sign 10: People Are Getting Sick

If you're noticing an uptick in sick time, late arrivals, early departures, doctor's appointments, or other reasons people use for avoiding tasks or meetings, pay attention early. This is an indicator of a stressed project team. Stressed teams don't complete tasks effectively. Invest time in figuring out with your team how to improve their work environment, or the project quality will suffer. More important, people's lives will suffer.

Adjusting Your Project

Your project will struggle at some point and may struggle the entire way. As manager, you must make strategic choices to get the project back on track. If you wait for problems to be fixed magically on their own, your project will fail. You must acknowledge and address change, or choices will be made for you.

In Step 2 you documented the starting constraints of the project. When the project begins to struggle, it's a good idea to revisit the constraints with all the sponsors to see if anything has changed that will reorder the constraint priorities. If the #1 constraint is still the top priority, you won't be able to negotiate any more of it. Instead, negotiate the #2 or #3 constraint with the sponsor.

Any project may be plagued by one or more of these conditions:
1. It may be behind schedule.
2. It may be over budget.
3. It may be producing output of insufficient quality.
4. The scope may have increased without a corresponding increase in schedule or budget.

The solutions to those problems could be

1. increase the time
2. increase the budget
3. decrease the quality requirements
4. decrease the scope.

Let's take a closer look at those four solution options, starting with increasing the time. When companies establish dates for project completion, those dates may or may not be fixed in stone. There's an interesting dance that occurs in business: Sponsors may ask for very ambitious dates because they know the projects are always delivered late. If you need to ask for more time, the time to ask for it is not a week before the project is due. Ask as early as possible.

Perhaps a bigger budget is possible. Sometimes you can hire consultants or add staff when a project is underresourced. In general, however, adding people to a project that's already in trouble will *increase* your trouble. Having more people on a project team requires more communication. In his book *The Mythical Man-Month*, Frederick Brooks explains that some tasks can't be subdivided easily—for example, you can't hire nine women to have a baby in one month.

A third option might be to work faster and for more hours and to eliminate less-essential tasks. This is what novice project managers try to do under stress. This strategy usually risks the project quality. Working as hard as you can is not sustainable (remember Warning Sign 10). In addition, it's often true that the less-essential tasks that are skipped are related to audit and control activities or simply are things the project team doesn't enjoy. Skipping tasks like "testing" will result in poor output quality.

As a fourth option, you can decrease project scope by doing a smaller subset of the total project with the available time and budget. This is actually the sanest approach. If you can narrow the scope of a project, and deliver a smaller but still full-quality project on time, you can deliver the rest in subsequent releases. This is a common approach, but it only works if the scope was clear and shared at the very start of the project. Some project managers, however, use this approach as a crutch for poor estimating, and sponsors get pretty sick of hearing about releases after a while.

Pushing the Decision to the Sponsor

It's hard but important to remember that the project belongs to the sponsor, the person with the business need and the money. The project manager is the steward of the project, watching it, nurturing it, and taking care of it until it's completed. The planning, organizing, and controlling of the project belong to the project manager. Unfortunately, project managers also make decisions every day about the future of their projects—decisions that should be made by the sponsor.

Project sponsorship requires establishing the business case for the project and then making the choice to invest, based on analysis of the return on that investment. Good sponsorship is not practiced enough in most companies, so it falls to the project manager to help the sponsor understand the imperatives of the role. More important, when project constraints or scope change, the manager must push choices with investment ramifications back to the person who owns them—the sponsor.

Let's say a project is running out of time and likely not to meet the deadline. The project manager has the options you read about above: deliver late (and likely over the budget), buy some help, deliver poor quality, or reduce the scope. Project management beginners make that decision on their own or with their team, but it's a decision that belongs to the sponsor. In many cases, here's what happens: The sponsor (or someone from her or his organization) requests that the manager increase the scope of the project, based on a change in the market. The sponsor, however, doesn't tell the project manager about the business market change. The project manager first grumbles and complains about how the sponsor is always changing her or his mind, and then sets off to increase the scope by stealing time from other project tasks, buying more resources, or neglecting quality.

As project manager, don't lose your sense of identity in the project—or your commitment to your appropriate responsibilities. And remember that the project belongs to someone else; it's simply on loan to you.

Communication

Figure 7.1 illustrates the findings of research done with IT projects. The results indicated that project managers who lie about their project status are likely to bring their projects in extremely late and over budget, if at all (on average 100 percent over budget). Project managers who tell the truth tend to bring the project in on time (if they keep their jobs). Why? Because telling the truth gets you the help you need before it's too late. Unfortunately, no one likes to deliver bad news upward, so the tendency to stretch the truth is very prevalent. Depending on corporate culture and politics, it may be necessary for you to pass project information to some other person who then will share it with the corporate sponsors. In that case, be sure to craft your communication in a clear and easily presentable form so that all the other person has to do is deliver the message. If your message isn't explicit and easy to grasp, you run the risk of playing project management "telephone," with your intermediary rephrasing and possibly misinterpreting what you're trying to say to your sponsors. If your news isn't good, there's a strong risk that the person you're depending on to deliver your project status report will join "The Liars Club" and minimize the bad news. Make sure your relationship with the intermediary helps him or her tell the truth.

Communicate early and often. I recently worked with a company that had aligned most of its resources with three critical and very large projects. The people on those project teams obviously had their hands full, especially with the political pressure on them. However, as I talked with people who were not involved with the critical projects, I learned they felt very left out. They were finding it impossible to secure the resources needed to get their own work done, and resources they thought they had often were swung over

FIGURE 7.1

Research Results: The Liars Club

The gray line indicates a typical "lying" project—one in which the real project status was not shared until it was too late. The black line indicates a typical "truth" project—one in which the real project status was shared early and often (and, early on, the project was late), but the truth provoked the focus that the project team needed to proceed successfully.

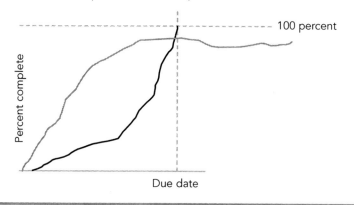

Source: http://web.mit.edu/jsterman/www/Liar%27s_club.html.

to the big projects with little or no prior notice. When I asked them how the big projects were going, and what they could do to help them be successful, they stared at me with blank looks on their faces. "Nobody tells us anything," they said.

It was an interesting learning experience for me. The success of the three mission-critical projects also depended on the individuals and teams who kept the operational side of the business going while the big projects were completed. They were stakeholders, but weren't being treated as such. No one thought of communicating with these people because they weren't directly associated with the project. The lesson for all project managers is to think of the public relations component when you're communicating project status. Think beyond those people who touch your project directly; remember the people whose buy-in may affect your project. How can you keep them enthusiastic and rooting for your success?

This is the point in the project when all the investment you have made in documenting the project will pay off. As change occurs—and it will—you'll have the information necessary to negotiate appropriate interventions. The deliverables themselves may change because they're artifacts of the life of the project. These deliverables include

1. the **Define** deliverables (Steps 1-5)—objectives, scope, risks, and constraints
2. the project schedule (Step 6)—the tasks, milestones, dependencies, and resource allocations
3. the key roles of project sponsor and subject-matter expert.

Each time one of these deliverables changes, communication must occur. The further into the project you are, the more updating and communication is necessary. For example, a change that affects the schedule most likely also affects the project objectives and scope.

What If I Skip This Step?

It would be nice—but impossible—to skip change. Making choices and implementing contingency plans will be done either by the project manager, or by neglect and default. A good manager owns these choices. He or she knows how to take the time to contemplate the project and think strategically, not just tactically. The warning signs are watched for and addressed. The project sponsor makes the business decisions, not the project manager. These are all critical behaviors for a project manager, and if change is ignored, the project will fail.

Lurking Landmines

◆   *The sponsor doesn't want to make any decisions and pushes everything to you.* First, be careful which decisions you push to the sponsor. The choices sent upward often are either too detailed or too broad. The sponsor should not be making decisions about detailed project tasks. Keep the sponsor's focus on the project's return-on-investment.

When problems arise, use your expertise to bring the sponsor your recommendations for solutions to the problem, but let the decision be made by the sponsor.

◆ *Something is unsettling, and you don't know what it is.* If you have a funny feeling about a project, it could be that inner voice. You can't hear the inner voice unless you stop long enough to listen and cut out the surrounding noise enough to hear. Practice the discipline of giving yourself the time, as frequently as risk dictates, to answer the question, Do I know where my project is?

Step 7 Checklist

✓ Watch for the warning signs of pending project disaster.
✓ Give yourself time to think about your project.
✓ Adjust your project, using the levers of time, money, quality, and scope.
✓ Push changes that affect the return-on-investment back to the rightful owner—the sponsor.

The Next Step

The next step will be about managing the people issues that can derail your project. In project management, it's always the people, so adapting to different communication styles and negotiating and managing conflict are key to project success.

STEP
7

Embrace the Natural Chaos of People

You've had it. The sponsor has delegated some key decisions to an important project stakeholder. You've left several voicemail messages and sent a slew of emails. These decisions are holding up your side of the project. You've even tried to catch her in the hall—to no avail. Today you're copied on an email she has sent to your executive sponsor, which says that the project is slipping because *you're* behind on your deliverable. What do you do? Quickly imagine the first three actions you'd take. Did any of these options come to mind?

◆ Call her immediately and leave a strong, angry message making it clear that you've been waiting for her and that she is the reason the project is late.

◆ Send an urgent email asking her to tell the sponsor the truth—you don't have what you need to proceed.

◆ Resend to her every email she hasn't responded to, and copy (that is, CC:) the executive sponsor just like she did.

◆ Go immediately to your boss and ask for help diffusing the situation.

STEP **8**

It was the sound

of pigs' feet that woke Demmy—pigs' feet trampling through the brushy edges of the clearing—and he had his door open long before his brothers got there. Neither Speedy nor Goldy had enough breath to speak when they skidded through the arch onto Demmy's soft grass floor. Demmy waited.

Finally, Speedy gasped out the bad news: "BB came and blew down our homes and we barely escaped with our little pig tails. We're so glad you built this strong brick house to protect us."

"Is that so?" Demmy asked, with more than a little irritation. "I've been expecting this all along, but you boys never really took the threat of the wolf seriously. With all the noise you were making, I'm sure BB's on his way here right now. I should just put you outside to face the fate you didn't figure on. Let BB chase you around and leave my house alone!"

It grew quiet in the house. Demmy considered his options. He wasn't so sure this house could keep the wolf out either. He'd run out of time and his great worry was that BB would see the wagon wasn't firmly attached. He could knock the wagon off the top and climb over the wall. Demmy glanced at his brothers. Speedy lay on his side, eyes already growing heavy. Goldy looked worried.

"Demmy, you're right," Goldy said softly. "I know I didn't take the wolf seriously, but I didn't have much money to spend. And Speedy got all wound up about his band idea. You've always been better at planning than either of us. But we're tuned in now, so what can we do to help?"

"Seems you've built a good structure here," Speedy chimed in. "Is there anything left to do? If we all work quickly, we can finish it up right before BB shows up."

Demmy looked up at the wagon-roof and back at his brothers.

"You know I love you guys," he said. "And I don't want any of us to be made into a BLT. There is something we can do to make this house safer."

He told them he'd been short of bricks to make a roof so he'd used the wagon weighted with the last few bricks to cover his house. Demmy was worried that the wagon wouldn't hold—that BB's gusty huffs would push it off and he'd climb in and snatch them. So together the brothers made a plan: When the wolf arrived, each little pig would grab hold of the wagon in a different place and use his weight to keep the wagon-roof in place. Weight was an advantage they had in common.

- Go to lunch with your friends and bemoan the fact that you have such an insane stakeholder.
- Look for a new job.

Before we talk about the best solution to such a problem, let's look at a couple facts about the situation:

- You're under pressure and your stakeholder is under pressure. In a stressed state, people often don't think clearly, understand each other, or say what they mean.
- Your piece of the project can't succeed without your stakeholder. She can't succeed without your help. The company can't succeed if the project falls apart.

Now let's look at the same situation from some different directions:

- It's possible that she thinks your requests for decisions are diabolical tactics to distract her from your inability to deliver project output. Maybe that happened to her before.
- Perhaps there was another way you could have gone on with the project when it became clear that you weren't getting what you needed. Maybe interim milestones could have been set up, or other people could have helped with the decision. Perhaps she wasn't as indispensable, and therefore as much of a roadblock, as you believed.
- Most important of all, there probably is something you could have done (or could do now) to make your nonresponsive stakeholder look good *and* meet your project goals successfully.

Communication is always the best bet and, as you learned in Step 5, collaboration is the most sensible strategy. Tool 8.1 offers some tips for reacting to negative feedback—and those tips will be helpful when you're communicating with a stakeholder with whom you're frustrated (and, apparently, a stakeholder who is frustrated with you).

In this step, you'll learn the project manager's most useful technique strategy—aligning the people involved with the success of the project, no matter what happens along the way. You'll learn

STEP **8**

TOOL 8.1

Ways to React When You Receive Negative Feedback

1. **Sort it out:** Ask a question starting with *what* or *how* to learn more about the situation in as calm a voice as possible. For example, ask, "What are the things I'm doing that you feel aren't working?" or "How do you feel I'm mismanaging the project?"

2. **Repeat:** Sometimes the best you can do when you're in total shock is say the same words back again. It's a little like the sort-it-out response, but you don't have to think of a *how* or *why* question. For example, simply saying, "I'm mismanaging the project?" gets the other person to continue talking while you recover your balance.

3. **Fog:** Get yourself a little space to calm down and think before anything else is said. If you're more comfortable face-to-face than on the phone, ask for a meeting. For example, make a suggestion like "Let's meet for coffee this afternoon and talk about this." If you prefer the telephone but need a few minutes to prepare to talk more easily, or if you and the caller aren't in the same office or country, say, "I want to give our conversation my full attention, so I must clear something off my desk before we talk. What's a good time for me to call you this afternoon?"

4. **Take a break:** If the conversation degrades to the point where it's going nowhere, take a break. For example, you might say, "I'm pretty emotional about this right now and need a little time to calm down. Let's set a time tomorrow to talk again and work toward a solution that meets both our needs."

---

how to negotiate with different stakeholders so that the project is successful. You'll continue to push the return-on-investment decisions back to the sponsors when appropriate.

Time to Complete This Step

The time you'll dedicate to working this step of your project will be proportional to the number of stakeholders on the project and to the corporate culture and politics. The more stakeholders are involved, the more differences of opinion you'll negotiate during project decision making. The amount of time a project manager has to spend defusing rivalries, negotiating conflicts, and the like is time that can't be spent in other management tasks. A project schedule can be affected.

Stakeholders

All the stakeholders may be involved in this step at some point in the project, but rarely at the same time. Each stakeholder will, of course, be very loyal to the area of the business for which she or he works. Although all want the project to be successful, each stakeholder will see the path to success from her or his unique business perspective. This creates conflict when tough scope or requirements decisions need to be made. Later in this step you'll learn how to

- Manage the conflict between stakeholders by identifying what is most important to each of them.
- Build a shared vision of success among stakeholders by mapping what each needs to the collaborative direction you'd like to take the project. Seek first to build consensus.

Questions to Ask

You can learn valuable information about the historical relationships of your stakeholders if you ask questions informally in the course of other conversations. For example:

- How long has each stakeholder been with the company?
- Where did each stakeholder work before?
- Gow long has each stakeholder been in his or her current position?
- What jobs has each held before?

And there are some vital questions that can't be asked outright because of their personal nature. Are there any important relationships about which you need to be aware—like strong ties to upper management. Are there current or prior marriages or partnerships that might affect the ways in which people work together. What history does everyone know, except you? I'm not encouraging you to be a gossip. As you display trustworthy behavior and convince people you're focused on the success of the project, other people will feel comfortable helping you understand the people dynamics. Any people who are personally competitive or don't get along before the project will use your project for their political chess game.

If one loses that game, everyone loses. You're the only one who can bring about a winning outcome for all involved.

Project Manager's Toolkit: Dealing with Conflict and Negative Feedback, and Negotiating Agreement

Let's tackle some techniques for managing conflict and negotiating agreement among warring factions. Effective communication will eliminate some conflict and need for negotiations, but not all of it. Even though your efforts in Steps 1–7 will help you establish a collaborative atmosphere on the project, you'll have plenty of opportunities to use the people-managing techniques described below. All projects come with stressful times that can light short fuses.

Start with How You Say It

The first place to improve effective communication is with your choice of words. When you're talking with someone else in a situation that may provoke discontent, choose your words wisely. Here are some important guidelines:

1. Speak from the perspective of *I* instead of *you*. For example, say "I feel that the project is struggling" instead of "You don't know, but the project is struggling."

2. Avoid *could, would, should* (often coupled with *you*). For example, avoid "You could have spent more time on it" or "I would have done that differently" or "You should have seen that coming."

3. Stick to the facts rather than your interpretations of the facts. For example, don't say "You meant to ruin my day." Try something like "Hearing today that the project is going to be five weeks late was difficult for me."

4. Avoid *but;* go with *and.* For example, saying "I heard what you said, but . . ." implies you don't care what the other person said—it's not as important as what you believe.

Replacing that with "I heard what you said, and . . ." implies you're listening and want to work together.

Consider this dialog:

Project Manager: Sorry I'm late. I'm so busy right now, I can barely get through the day. I really need your help.

Stakeholder: What can I help with?

Project Manager: Well, I really haven't had time to think of all the things. Really, you should know better than I do what are the critical steps to bring your department into alignment with the rest of the team. Your people seem to feel like they're too important to help us with this project. I just don't understand that.

Stakeholder: I'm not sure what you're talking about. We weren't supposed to begin our part of the project until next month, according to the original schedule.

Project Manager: You were the ones that made me put that in the schedule but no one wanted to confront you. I never wanted you to start that late. Your team should have been in place last month.

Contrast that with the following dialog:

Project Manager: I appreciate your taking the time to meet with me today. I need some help, and I'm hoping I can get some help from your department.

Stakeholder: What can I help with?

Project Manager: Although the project schedule originally said your team would get involved next month, I've found that the project team needs your expertise as soon as we can get it. I believe your people have a perspective that will help us now, and avoid rework later in the year on this project.

Stakeholder: I'm not sure I can get all those people free. We weren't expecting to allocate headcount until next month.

Project Manager: I'm sure it's a surprise and that's why I wanted to talk with you directly. I'd appreciate any help you could get us—even a couple of people would be great.

STEP 8

The first dialog comes from a project manager who is only concerned with his or her own perspective. The second dialog comes from a project manager who knows that the project can only be successful if everyone is onboard. Simple word changes can make the difference between a successful project and a conflict-ridden overdue project.

Bad News Early Is Good News

Healthy conflict is good and serves an important purpose on a project. Here are a couple of its advantages:

- it clarifies confused or ill-defined objectives, scope, or roles
- it triggers innovative problem solving and agility.

In fact, if there's no conflict evident, you can be almost sure that there are people who are afraid to voice their opinions. It also means that your team is taking the easy way out. Projects with teams holding information back are always late and exceed their budgets. When people don't bring conflict to the surface, problems don't come out until it's very late in the game—and that means help isn't available until it's too late.

In the best situations, bad news revealed by conflict early on really *is* good news. It's your task to create a climate that doesn't discourage debate and disagreement. Model for your team the behaviors that show you are able and willing to turn conflict into a tool that will be used with everyone's safety in mind. In this way, from the outset everyone involved in your project will feel OK about bringing up their issues because they know you'll work to resolve them effectively. Clarify whatever misunderstandings exist and encourage innovative collaboration and communication to solve disagreements. Resolve small conflicts as soon as they arise, before they morph into wars.

Ways to React to Negative Feedback

Bad news won't always create conflict. It can be something that just happens and is no one's fault. Another type of interruption is negative feedback. This is when someone on your project team or

It's Not Personal

The conflict that circles you on a critical project has a lot to do with the perceived importance of the endeavor—and very seldom anything to do with you as a human being. Conflict isn't personal assault. Although your initial reaction to someone's expression of disagreement may be one of hurt feelings or anger, take a breath. React to the issues, not the person, as much as possible.

one of your stakeholders criticizes something you're doing on the project.

Consider how you react when someone gives you criticism about your project management choices. Do you get angry? Do you punish the messenger in some way? As in the scenario I sketched for you at the start of this step, do you throw your energy into fighting the criticism rather than working through it?

Each piece of criticism contains a nugget of truth that the project manager must address. Either the criticism is accurate and the project has to be adjusted, or it's inaccurate and the person delivering the critique must be influenced in a positive way that gets him or her back onboard. Still, it's hard to be objective about criticism in the moment, and it's hard to get your initial physical reaction under control before you respond.

Imagine that one of your stakeholders has called and said to you, "You're mismanaging the project." Tool 8.1 showed four types of responses you can make during the initial shock of hearing bad project feedback. No matter which tack you take, follow these pointers for success:

STEP 8

- Don't be defensive; avoid taking the feedback personally.
- Acknowledge the feelings of the person giving you the negative feedback; people sometimes just want to be heard.
- Do not apologize unless you have done something that has caused the problem. There's a difference between empathizing ("I can see this is really bothering you") and apologizing ("I'm sorry I did that").

◆ Express regret about the situation, saying something like "I'm sorry you feel I haven't managed the project well." (See how that statement differs from an apology?)

◆ Find an area of agreement. Point out that both of you want the same thing for the project, which is usually true. Any small thing that you can agree on is a great start.

◆ Suggest alternatives and solutions. Continue to try different approaches tied to the needs that have been expressed by the negative feedback.

Ways to Deliver Negative Feedback

Sometimes the tables are turned and you have to deliver criticism to a key stakeholder or subject-matter expert—for example, the quality of his work may be inadequate or her deliverables may be late repeatedly. Doing so requires some planning to be successful. Tool 8.2 gives you some tips for successfully delivering unpopular, but necessary and constructive feedback.

Using concise, clear language will help ensure that a difficult conversation doesn't escalate or have to be repeated, and that the outcome is productive. It's very tempting during conflict to hurry through the conversation in a rush to be done with it, gloss over

TOOL 8.2
Tips for Delivering Negative Feedback

1. Determine exactly what you want the outcome of your communication with the stakeholder to be. How will you measure that the communication has been successful?

2. Think about the person you'll communicate with—what's important to that person? How can your message build on that? How will she or he measure that your meeting has been successful?

3. Determine what points you must make to get the outcome you want.

4. Determine what you will do if you don't get your desired outcome. What will you accept? What will you not accept?

TOOL 8.3

The Four Fs of Successful Feedback

The following four terms should describe any message you communicate to your stakeholders and team members:

1. **Factual** (versus hearsay or interpretation): Data are accurate, specific, clear, and observable.

2. **Free of emotion** (versus angry): Your tone is calm, neutral, free of rancor.

3. **Fresh** (versus outdated): The event you're talking about happened recently.

4. **Forward action focused** (versus fault focused): The next action to be taken is discussed or explained; it's clearly defined, achievable, and measurable.

---

the message, or leave out critical elements. Use the four Fs in tool 8.3 to keep your words clear and your feedback effective. Planning what you want to say and how you want to say it before you engage in a difficult conversation can keep you from losing lots of time to entrenched conflict later.

Five Steps to Negotiating

When there's a difference of opinion, whether it involves you or only other parties to the project, you may have to play the role of negotiator to bring the sparring partners back together. Figure 8.1 shows a process for negotiation that leads toward a win/win solution. Call a meeting and follow these steps:

1. **Go to the balcony:** As conflict unfolds, remember that you are not the project—you are the steward of the project. In your mind, go above the conflict and watch it from the balcony. Pretend it's only a movie. Who are the people in conflict? What do they really want? Watch the characters and learn from the clues what each is asking for.

2. **Stay on topic:** As often as needed, bring the discussion back to the main issue(s). Clarify what the conflict con-

FIGURE 8.1

Five Steps to Successful Negotiating

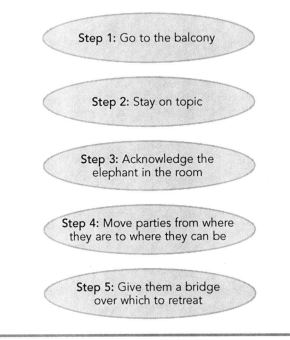

Step 1: Go to the balcony

Step 2: Stay on topic

Step 3: Acknowledge the elephant in the room

Step 4: Move parties from where they are to where they can be

Step 5: Give them a bridge over which to retreat

Source: Adapted from Roger Fisher and William Ury, and Bruce Patton, *Getting to Yes: Negotiating Agreement without Giving In* (New York: Penguin Books, 1981).

cerns and what the point of the meeting is. Keep people from expanding the scope of the disagreement. Stick to the topic at hand so a solution can be created. Be the owner of the meeting agenda and stay on task.

3. **Acknowledge the elephant in the room:** If there is something that people are *not* saying and you know that it's relevant to the conflict, call it out. Speak the words that everyone else can't say. There is a magic to speaking aloud something that others are saying to themselves in their heads. When it's visible, people can deal with it.

4. **Move parties in conflict from where they are to where they can be** (small steps): Each person has unique values

and strengths, and each person views the project from a different context. Conflict can come from this uniqueness because perspectives can be so different. This is the kind of conflict that can create great innovation. For you as a negotiator, however, this means that the same approach won't work for everyone. You'll need to listen deeply to each of the players and try to understand his or her unique viewpoint. Only then can you determine how far each person is willing and able to move. Negotiating is not easy to do in a team setting, so you may need a break to collect your thoughts and strategize before the final negotiation.

5. **Give them a bridge over which to retreat:** What do you do with the person who refuses to budge even when all the evidence indicates the position she or he holds is not productive? When a person refuses to collaborate, no matter what anyone says or does, it generally doesn't mean that he or she is ignorant of the logic; it means he or she is resisting it. It's critical that you give this person a way to retreat safely. In other words, you'll have to come up with a way to make it seem like the solution was his or her idea. Find a way for the resistor to agree and save face.

Be warned: For some power-trippers, there are times when it's more important to argue than to build consensus. You may *not* be able to negotiate consensus with everyone. This is another reason strong sponsorship is so important—let the sponsor break the tie if there's no other way to get it done.

Conflict and Different Reactive Behaviors

Different types of people react to conflict in different ways. It's important to understand why they're reacting in that manner so you can adapt to their perspective and build collaboration. Let's consider four types of people you'll find in almost any organization—the executive, the people-oriented worker, the team-oriented worker, and the highly technical person—and see how they behave in conflict.

The Executive in Conflict

Executives are concerned about movement. They measure success by what gets done. Tasks and speed are critical to them. If a project seems to slow down their chance of getting tasks done quickly, they'll be very angry, and the anger most likely will be directed at the project manager.

Leveraging that accomplishment-oriented focus, project managers can negotiate ways to get more project help. An executive wants to be told what the project manager intends to do (tasks) and by when (quickly) to get the project back on track. Don't bore her with details of how the project got where it is, and don't ask her to solve the problems for you. Follow the executive's gaze forward. After sharing your solution factually and briefly, let her know what you need from her to make that solution viable.

Executives react very positively to discussions that involve return-on-investment. They're comfortable speaking in those terms. Make sure your solution creates a strong return for the project investment, and that you clearly articulate that return for the executive.

The People-oriented Person in Conflict

There are cheerleaders in your company who have lots of alliances, make a lot of noise, and move quickly to gain more support. Because they're so strongly networked, they are stakeholders that you can't discount. With their powerful influencing skills, these people can produce a coup on your project team if their conflict issues aren't dealt with early.

Under stress and in times of change, the people-oriented person can feel hurt and may withdraw. Such behavior disturbs her or his network and people along that network adopt the same behavior in support of the upset party. It's lucky for you that bringing the people-person and her or his network back in sync with the project is a simple task.

Have a face-to-face discussion with your people-person and reiterate how important this project is to the company. Explain to him (and believe) that you can't hit the project goals without his help. Ask his advice about how to adapt to other people who are involved in the conflict (his sympathetic network). The people-focused person can be a tremendous asset to you if you're not as naturally gifted with influencing skills.

The Team-oriented Person in Conflict

Research has shown that nearly 40 percent of the people in your company like to be part of a team. They care about finishing projects. These are the individuals who seek to keep everyone involved and focused, following the processes, and doing the work. Because their focus is on teamwork, change of any kind can create conflict in their world—and conflict is the principal thing they want to avoid at all costs.

When team-centered people are stressed, it's very difficult to tell that anything is wrong. They still try to keep the team together, and sometimes agree to do things when they're really just being supportive. In times of stress, other people on the team may see the team-oriented person as someone who doesn't deliver what she promises. At the same time, that person doesn't think she promised anything because she was just voicing support.

When you see this dynamic occurring on your team, spend some time with your team-centered person. Reinforce the critical role she plays on the project. Ask questions that give her the opportunity to let you know what's causing her stress and fear. Talk through the reality of the situation and help her see the best way to move forward. Usually it helps to work out the first couple of things to do together and then let her figure out the rest on her own.

The Highly Technical Specialist in Conflict

These people are important to a project because sometimes they can't be replaced easily. A computer programmer or an engineer, for example, will have expertise in the project work that few others can help them with or even understand. Many of these people tend toward perfectionism. Their work is tightly tied to their sense of self, and

Micromanagement

As a good leader, try not to "fix" conflict for others. Instead, coach them to solve the problem themselves whenever you can (see Step 5). Under the pressure of project work, it's tempting to micromanage every little conflict because you think it will help the project. *It doesn't.* Strong, smart project managers may jump in and fix things so often that the teams learn to depend on them for every decision. At first, this team dependency may stroke the manager's ego, but if every project decision—no matter how small—has to clear the manager, the project will take much longer than it should. Learn to grow the expertise of your people, not replace it.

they almost always need more time to make things perfect. Unfortunately, few projects have unlimited extra time. Many technical specialists will always report being "90 percent done," even when they're not under the kind of unusual project stress that conflict produces.

The tech guy will test your deadlines from the start. To get more time, he will redirect your attention away from his work toward something else that will keep you busy while he pursues his definition of perfection. That's a behavior I describe as "setting a fire on the other side of the room."

As the project manager, you can't avoid addressing time issues with the technical person. Meet face-to-face and explain—specifically and in terms of measures—what behavior you need from him, what output he must deliver by what time, and the consequences if those goals aren't met. Stay the course and don't fall for any attempted redirection. When you put these concrete boundaries in place, your relationship with the technical specialist will be easier.

To take a macro viewpoint of those four types of people, their behavioral styles in stressful situations are, respectively,

- ◆ urgent, task-oriented
- ◆ urgent, people-oriented
- ◆ diligent, team-oriented
- ◆ diligent, quality-oriented

If you have trouble deciding which preferences you're dealing with, you're safest if you assume the preference is for diligence. Take plenty of time to explain your project, the schedule, and your strategy (this will appeal to the quality- and task-oriented worker). Then explain how the conflict affects the team (this will be important to the team- and people-oriented worker).

The Importance of Listening Deeply

An important project management skill is hearing what actually is being said. With all the chaos around projects, it's hard to focus on one person at a time, but listening deeply is the only way you can be sure you hear. Tool 8.4 offers tips to use when listening to make sure you have the focus you need.

Communication

Handling conflict requires communication. Your original communication plan is probably not going to be adequate for the people-issue surprises that occur when change strikes. As a project manager, you'll be required to practice "communications improv"—being able to provide feedback through good listening skills and effective word choices. If scope, budget, or timelines change, return to the documents and update them so everyone knows about the change. Specifically, balance the need to move quickly with the need to move well by keeping your eye on

- ◆ the **Define** deliverables, including objectives, scope, risks, and constraints
- ◆ the **Plan** deliverables, including the schedule with associated resource allocations
- ◆ the key roles, including project sponsor, stakeholders, project team, and subject-matter experts.

Pay attention to the way you communicate with your sponsors. There will be some you like more than others—that's natural. But treating people differently will only increase the conflict. For example, there is a symbolism to meeting with one sponsor face-to-face in his or her office and another in a group setting. Meeting one-on-one may give the impression that this sponsor is more important

TOOL 8.4

Listening Tips

* Face the person. Make eye contact. Stop whatever you're doing and focus on the person speaking.

* Use *active* listening—repeat and rephrase what is being said and test that you understand what is being said.

* Inside your head, a little voice (called *self-talk*) will be talking to you about what you're going to say next. Sometimes you can be so busy planning your next remark that you don't hear what has just been said. To manage your self-talk, it may help to jot a quick note to yourself and then refocus. It's even better to just tune out the self-talk and trust that, when the time comes, you'll know what to say.

* Make sure you listen to everything the person has said before jumping to problem solving. If you're a person who likes to move quickly, it might be difficult to be patient while another person finishes his or her thoughts. Continue to refocus on the words being said.

* If possible, ask questions that help the speaker figure out how to solve the problem himself or herself. There's a classic *Harvard Business Review* article about monkeys: When a person comes into your office, there usually are monkeys on his back. Your goal is to see that he leaves with all the monkeys he brought in. Reflect back to the individual what you've heard, and ask questions rather than offering a solution. For example, "What I hear you saying is that your project assignments are going to be late. What are some ways that you can make up the time?" Notice the question was *not* "What are some ways I can help you make up the time?"

---

than the other. Be aware of how power is measured in the corporate culture in which you're operating. Something as simple as having lunch rather than having coffee with a person prompts different interpretations of respect.

What If I Skip This Step?

If you avoid conflict or let it run its course, the project will fail to meet its original goals. The conflict will escalate into a major explosion, usually at some point near the end of the project. Relationships will be broken beyond repair, which will have an impact on future projects. In fact, there's no way to skip this step. Conflict will hunt you down—you may run, but you can't hide.

Lurking Landmines

◆ *There's a conflict between two members of the team that has been carried forward to your project.* Get the details and make sure you have your facts straight. Talk to each of the parties one-on-one. If possible, negotiate a discussion about how they can best work together on this project. If it requires them staying apart, that's fine as long as they both agree. Don't get into the previous conflict, and don't try to figure out whose fault it was. That never works.

◆ *You've overheard project team members speaking in sarcastic terms about subject-matter experts or sponsors.* This is an important leadership challenge. As the leader, you must make clear that this is inappropriate and unhelpful behavior. Make sure you aren't modeling some of this language yourself when you get stressed with a difficult stakeholder. There's no need to create more conflict by being angry or dictatorial, so sell to the team the reasons for keeping communication open.

◆ *You're starting to feel like it's you against your team. They stop talking when you enter the room.* Create a strategic enemy for your team to unite around so they won't turn on you, or on one another. For example, during the rollout of the original Macintosh at Apple, the team focused on Microsoft as its enemy. What enemy could your team compete against that would not hurt the company direction or your project goals? How can you redirect the competitive energies from an inappropriate enemy to an engaging one? Nothing unites a team like competition against an "outsider."

Step 8 Checklist

✓ Manage conflict well to improve project success. Bad news early is good news.

✓ Use negative feedback to improve the project. When receiving negative feedback, remember that there's always a nugget of truth in it. When delivering, make sure you're clear about what outcome you want and use appropriate language.

✓ Be prepared to negotiate conflict between the people important to your project.

✓ Adapt your behaviors to the different needs of different people on your project team. Help them continue to support the progress of the project.

✓ Listen, really listen. Make the time for people to communicate with you. Move away from the keyboard!

The Next Step

Your next step is to finish the project. It's amazing, but one of the most difficult parts of a project can be ending it.

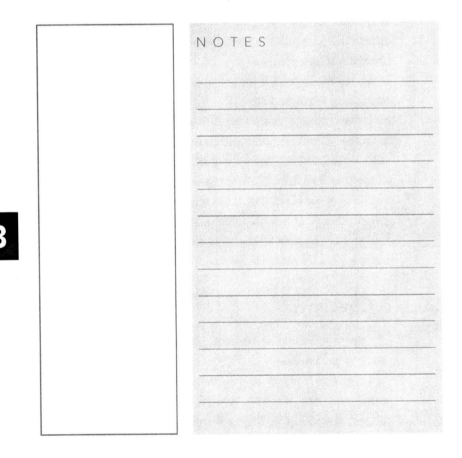

NOTES

Know When You're Done

Documents That
Substantiate Completion

Process for Ending Well

Transfer of the Project

Celebration!

Ending a project—sometimes called "closing"—occurs when the project sponsors accept the project deliverables. Sometimes this can be quite formal, with a sign-off, but often it's less dramatic.

The time to talk about finishing well is not at the end. If you've skipped earlier steps, it's unlikely that you'll finish well. Even if you've done everything well, it's still more difficult than you'd think to end a project. During the project, you're under tremendous pressure from sponsors to hit your due dates, but when the final due date has arrived, some sponsors don't want the project to end. Suddenly they want to add every requirement they can imagine.

Projects today are increasingly complex, time constrained, and unclear. Change is the norm, not the exception. People who don't take the time to create the deliverables of the **Define** and **Plan** phases are doomed to do free overtime work.

We recently had the opportunity to develop a sales training initiative. This project involved training, coaching, mentoring, assessment, process design, and compliance. It was a wonderful chance to

Each little pig was ready.

Goldy and Demmy took the sides and Speedy held the wagon firm at the back corner. It wasn't long before wolf breath stirred the trees. Not one little pig eye blinked. Even the jingle of Speedy's cell phone didn't break their concentration. Each pig held his part of the wagon as tight as he could.

"Little pigs, little pigs, let me in!" BB bellowed. But the only movement was six firmer grips.

A small wolf-scented wind became a mighty huff and a mightier puff. It blew in between the bricks but the walls stood firm. A pause, and the pigs felt the weight of the wolf on the wagon-roof. Now his huffs and his puffs pushed the wagon more firmly into place. The pigs and the walls held firm.

Finally the wind stopped, and the pigs heard the wolf's tired voice. "OK, you win. I can't blow this house down. Anybody want to get breakfast?"

Demmy thought a moment and then called through the door, "BB, we're tired of running from you, and we're tired of building things for you to knock down. Can we all agree to stop?"

"That would be great," said the wolf, blowing out a big sigh. "I really don't enjoy this anymore. I'd like to retire, maybe do some volunteer work. Something that doesn't wear me out so much. It's time for us all to move on to other things. You have my word."

Demmy looked at his brothers, and all nodded their heads. He opened the door and the three little pigs walked out into the quiet dawn. Each pig shook BB's paw and a deal was struck to end this chapter of their lives.

practice performance consulting, influencing every aspect of a company's approach to sales. The program, to be rolled out to 100 sales managers across the country, would take 18 months to deliver.

The client's chief financial officer was a shrewd negotiator. As we worked out the final pricing and requirements for our contract, he asked that we share the risk of successfully completing the project. His offer was that I risk 25 percent of the total contract amount on their reaching a specific increase in sales, although it was clear at the start what the timeframe would be for that metric. The target increase was moderate, but if their sales team didn't achieve it, I'd have to return to them one quarter of a large dollar amount in services. Normally, a training class is not enough to guarantee increases in sales, but this time we weren't just creating and delivering a class. We were going to work on the entire sales function with them. I thought about the offer and agreed, with the following constraints in the contract:

- ◆ the subject-matter experts would be available to us at least 10 hours a week.
- ◆ low-performing sales representatives would be let go if they couldn't adapt to the new sales processes.
- ◆ sales growth would be measured after 18 months (that is, 36 months after the start of the project). I negotiated for 36 months because I believed that if the training was successful and the constraints of the project were honored, sales would go down during the transition to the new processes. With any change, there are people who are just unable or unwilling to make the move.

As the project progressed, the scope fluctuated, sales regulations changed, and corporate executives were shuffled. Through it all, the project went well. There were many advantages to this shared-risk approach to projects, including executive buy-in to do everything necessary to support the change. The project constraints I requested were honored, which drove the success of the project. The sales went up after the first class and continued to go up as the processes evolved and new training was done throughout the 18 months. The sales numbers exceeded the "deal" by the 36-month point. In retrospect, I wish I'd put some bonus money in the contract for achieving the high results in addition to sharing the risk.

As I think about that project now, I believe that negotiating this unique contract in the beginning, especially the shared risk component, ensured that all parties involved knew exactly how we were going to measure the end of the project. There were deliverables at certain milestones—process redesign, three rounds of instructor-led training, e-learning components, and redesigned job responsibilities—but the most critical goal was that sales increased by a specific amount within 36 months. In the absence of such a concrete understanding reached with the sponsor before the project starts, a project manager has to find some way to describe a final deliverable—an outcome, a product, a process, something tangible or measurable that means "our work is over here" when it's transferred from the project manager to the sponsor. As a project nears the end of its schedule, emotions are high, needs have changed, and it's a bad time to make agreements you should have reached at the beginning.

Stakeholders

The stakeholders of the project are again the key players in determining what the "end" will look like. The most important stakeholders are your project sponsors. Because the project is being funded by them, they'll decide how to measure the successful completion.

Your stakeholders are just like everyone else. They aren't completely clear about what they want at the beginning of a project, but they'll know it when they see it. The communication patterns that you've established from the beginning pay off at the end. Clearly described project deliverables and timeframes all along make it less likely that a stakeholder will change the deliverables and timeframes at the end.

Still, business change does occur, and often at a less-than-ideal time. Even as the project ends, sponsors retain the right to ask for changes, more requirements, and anything else they want because it is their project. Your response as project manager is, "Yes, we can do that, and it will cost $X and take X more weeks to deliver." The scope diagram you constructed in an earlier step will serve as proof to everyone concerned that those requests are new and that they aren't covered by the budget, time, and human resources previously granted to the project. If you skipped creating a diagram earlier, create one now.

There may be stakeholders who've agreed with (or, at least, ignored) the objectives, scope, and progress to this final point, but now find major problems. Remember what you've learned about communication, conflict, and collaboration. It may be that their last-minute dissatisfaction arises more from a need to be heard and acknowledged than from a serious need for project changes. Listen to their concerns, work toward a collaborative outcome, and find a safe bridge over which these people can retreat. Compromises and consensus are always possible if you're willing to be patient and wait it out.

As the implementation of the project deliverables approaches, specifically spell out the following for your stakeholders:
- what will be delivered
- when it will be delivered
- to whom it will be delivered
- what stakeholders' role(s) will be.

Even if these same tasks have been part of the project schedule all along, it's critical that you spend time managing the expectations of the stakeholders as you move into the final lap.

Your executive sponsor and other participants who exhibit the dominance behavioral mode will lose interest in the project as it nears completion. These people like to start things; they get bored with the endings. It will be difficult to keep them involved until the end. If your project is going well, they'll lose interest. If your project is going poorly, they'll try to take it over and fix it. Vary your communication to keep their interest, sharing successes and challenges and explaining what you'll do about those challenges.

This effort will keep their interest in the project and their trust in you.

Influencers also will be on to other things. They lose interest because they feel the project is a done deal long before the end is official. Keeping them tuned in will be difficult, but you'll need their evangelist approach to get everyone through the transition. Put the influencer in charge of creating the celebration.

Most of the members of your project team and most stakeholders will be steady types. These people prefer the status quo. They're comfortable working on the project, and they grow nervous about what will happen to everyone when the project ends. Keep up communication with them and be certain they always have a clear list of tasks. Staying focused on the daily work of the project will help them move through the uncertainty.

The perfectionist compliant person doesn't want the project to end because it's never quite right. This person usually is one of your technical or subject-matter experts. Although perfection is a nice ideal, it's not cost feasible. You'll have to push your perfectionists to finish the tasks they've been assigned—especially at the end.

Questions to Ask

Ask the stakeholders the following questions as you prepare to end the project:

- When would you like to set up the acceptance meeting?
- Who will need to be present at the acceptance meeting?
- Who will track the features that were not included in this project? How will these features/aspects be handled (for example, maintenance releases)?
- Who will be the person responsible for the project deliverables after delivery? What will the hand-off period be?
- When will the project team resources be released to other project work?

Project Manager's Toolkit: Documents to Define, Declare, and Substantiate Completion

Tool 9.1 lists and describes the documentation you need to have in place to complete the project. Those documents describe the objectives and scope of the work to be completed. If you haven't created and updated these documents as you've moved through the project steps, you can't substantiate the close—you can't prove that you've delivered to the sponsor all that was required of you and you can't get the sponsor's final sign-off. As a starting point in this step, open your project file and make sure you have all the documents listed in tool 9.1 and that all of them are current. Late in the project, when you can see the light at the end of the tunnel, it's tempting to let the documentation get a little obsolete. Use this tool to refresh your own memory of these deliverables, and invest the time to bring them up to date.

Depending on the conflict that occurred during the project, it may be difficult to end the project with a sponsor, and difficult to get her or him to sign off on the final output. This is another reason that your documentation needs to be in good shape. Make sure there have been updates to your project schedule to show the output delivered to the stakeholders, the date(s) it was delivered, and the person or department that received it.

In addition, future project managers may use your project documentation to help them create and maintain their project deliverables. Libraries of project documentation provide a tremendous benefit to newer project managers, and a great way for project knowledge management to be extended within an organization.

Notice that the entire project schedule is *not* one of these substantiating documents. Although it's useful while the project is in progress, it's only post-project value is as a historical record of the project and as a tool in the post-project review. Occasionally, the actual times for some tasks on the project schedule may be useful to defend project decisions that you made—for example, noting

STEP 9

that requirements from a stakeholder were not delivered on time and that delayed the implementation. Most stakeholders don't want to review this level of detailed history; and, for the project manager, this level of debate is usually better avoided because of the conflict it creates.

TOOL 9.1

Your Project's Substantiating Documentation

As your project draws to a close, make certain you have all your project documentation on file. There are two purposes for ensuring that the documentation is complete and that you know where it is:

1. If there is a disagreement about a deliverable that was not part of the implementation, the documentation can provide explanation.

2. These documents describe the project in a way that defines the end, and therefore will help you secure your sponsor's final sign-off.

Here are the documents you should have:

- **Business Objectives:** This is a statement of the ways in which this project will increase revenue, avoid or decrease costs, improve service, satisfy regulatory requirements, and/or keep up with changes in the industry and with strides made by the competition.

- **Project Objectives:** This document describes the specific output that the project will produce and explains how you and your sponsor will measure that output so that the project endpoint is apparent to all parties.

- **Scope Diagram:** The diagram is a graphic enumeration of the project stakeholders and a depiction of the flow of input and output to and from the project. It illustrates the outer edges of the project, clearly depicting the end product(s) to be delivered. It establishes lines of responsibility and shows what ancillary actions/interactions are not within the scope of the project.

- **Risk Assessment:** This document, based on each stakeholder's individual assessment of the project's inherent risk (in terms of size, requirement stability, resources, and technology), establishes the likely level and source(s) of risk the project will encounter.

- **Constraints Statement:** This statement defines the forces that will restrict or compel various aspects of the project—forces that generally focus on time, budget, and quality.

- **Assumptions:** This document is a list of underlying assumptions about resources, expert knowledge, processes, and technology you and the project team will need to perform the work of the project.

STEP 9

TOOL 9.2

Criteria Describing the Project's End

* **Scope:** The project inputs and where they will come from, and the project outputs (deliverables) and who will receive them

* **Business case and objectives:** The financial goals the successful project will meet, generally focused on improving service, avoiding cost, increasing revenue, or reacting to government regulations

* **User acceptance testing:** The results of the stakeholders' testing of the system prior to full implementation, including test cases and logs of results

* **User sign-off:** The sign-off of the project sponsors based on the results of the user acceptance testing

* **Letter of completion:** A formal communication to all stakeholders explaining the end of the project and the timing of the transition to maintenance

* **Project documentation archive:** The location of the project documentation for future use

A Process for Ending Well

How do you know when you're done? On what criteria will you and your sponsor base your agreement that you've reached the end? Your organization may have standard steps for ending a project if it has a formal project management or development method. If not, take a look at tool 9.2, which lists criteria on which you can make your agreement.

Just as there is a stepwise process for doing the work of a project, there's a process for ending it—and ending it well. Tool 9.3 describes the four steps of that process. The steps are fairly formal, but they ensure that everyone knows that the project is completed and all acceptance is documented. Because delivering input to a project team member's performance review, formally closing contracts with external suppliers, and getting official closure from the sponsors may involve difficult conversations, some project managers avoid that work or do it casually. Taking that path doesn't serve you, your sponsors, or your team members well.

STEP 9

TOOL 9.3

Step-by-Step Process for Ending a Project

Step and Activity	Description	Stakeholder(s) Responsible
1–Determine if the project is done	Measure project performance and deliverables: • Evaluate the deliverables' quality and the extent to which it satisfies the project's requirements • Decide whether the project's objectives were achieved • Determine whether the benefits documented as part of the business objective were realized	All
2–Evaluate team performance	Evaluate the performance of the project team members: • Gather and analyze relevant performance metrics, including feedback for job performance reviews • Provide performance feedback for each member of the project team	Project manager
3–Close the contract(s)	When third parties have been contracted to provide products or services to the project team: • Determine whether the third-party vendor has satisfied all contractual obligations, according to the contract terms and conditions • Formally notify the third-party vendor that the contract is complete	External vendors, project manager
4–Obtain project acceptance	Obtain formal project acceptance: • Document the results of the user acceptance testing • Get the signature of the project sponsor on the document stating that the project is complete	Executive sponsor, project manager

To complete the steps of the ending process, make certain you have all the documentation listed and described in tool 9.4. The requisite documents will substantiate decisions and changes made

TOOL 9.4

Documents Archived as You End the Project

Material	Details and Remarks
Approved business case	The approved business case, including business objectives, is required to assess the project and determine whether the identified benefits were realized. This material was created in the **Define** phase and was modified as needed, with the approval of the project sponsors during the **Plan** and **Manage** phases.
Approved project management schedule	Specific tasks and due dates set forth in the project schedule are used to evaluate each team member's performance and to substantiate feedback provided by the project manager for the individual's performance review.
Product/service documentation	Whatever thorough documentation is expected to accompany the delivery of the final product or service, including • requirements and technical specifications • system guides and manuals • service-level agreements.
Performance and status reports	These are the reports the project manager has compiled and sent to sponsors and stakeholders throughout the course of the project. These reports will also contribute to performance reviews.
Contract documents	Any external contract documentation, including • the contract itself, with all supporting and referenced materials • the contractor project deliverables, correspondence, invoices, and payment records • audit results, if applicable.
Updated project tracking spreadsheet(s) and risk log	This is the final set of project tracking spreadsheets (including issues, decisions, and deliverables for review/approval), and the risk log. These materials will help the manager track changes that occurred in project deliverables and, thus, will contribute to performance reviews.

STEP 9

during the project, and will be very useful supporting data for compiling workers' performance reviews and for conducting the eventual post-project review.

Finally, secure the sponsor's signed acknowledgment of receipt and formal approval of the project's promised output. See tool 9.5 for the list of materials to be gathered and archived as a record of project completion. All of your stakeholders should know that these materials have been compiled and where and how they can view or get copies of them if necessary.

Turning Over the Project

When a project is completed, the work of maintaining it is shifted to the business area of the organization. The transition involves a lot of effort. Don't assume that the project will be taken over easily by the business area. If the business area hasn't really considered

TOOL 9.5

Documents That Declare a Project Complete

Material	Details and Remarks
Project definition	This includes the project objectives and/or contracts that defined early in the project what project approval would be based on.
Closure report	This report documents the results of user acceptance testing.
Project sign-off	This is a document signed by the project sponsors that states that the project is complete.
Project archives	The project archive includes • all project documentation—plans, logs, and reports • explanatory documentation for the products/services delivered—requirement specifications, technical specifications, manuals, and guides • contract documentation—contacts, product deliverables, invoices, and audit results (when performed).

who'll take up whatever the project produced and delivered, you'll probably get some pushback from the recipient department.

As project manager, you're stuck at this point between two worlds. You're still getting calls requesting tweaks to the project, even though it's complete, but you've moved on to other work. Weeks before the transition, use the tools in this step to start managing the hand-off expectations of the business area. Explain how it will be done—and when. Involve the sponsor in all the communications about ending.

It may be necessary to escalate to the sponsor if the transition activities don't occur. Handle this carefully by sharing with the sponsor the date you'll no longer be involved. Also offer ideas for who might pick up the slack on the business side. Leverage the negotiation tips covered in Step 8.

Celebrate!

At the end of the project, acknowledge and celebrate the team's accomplishments. Doing so gives everyone a sense of satisfaction, recognition, and closure. When you decide how to celebrate, make sure that all stakeholders have the opportunity to participate in the festivities. Don't leave out anyone, no matter how small his or her role was in the overall scheme.

Communication

It's tempting to cut back the communication a bit when the end is in sight. *Don't make that mistake.* Continue sending out your project status spreadsheets, showing progress, and keeping the end visible to everyone. Be very clear about end dates, including those for testing and implementation plans when those are part of the project. If possible, set the dates and build the stakeholders' anticipation of their involvement in the post-project review, which we'll address in Step 10.

Communication must be very explicit at the hand-off point. There are three possible transition scenarios:

1. Individual stakeholders will be responsible going forward for the new processes, the technology, and the other deliverables of the project.
2. Multiple stakeholders will be responsible for everything, but the ownership is unclear.
3. No one has been assigned to take care of the deliverables from your project.

Having a single person responsible for a project deliverable is the best option. For example, one IT person takes responsibility for maintaining the software, and one functional manager maintains the process. In such a case, what you need to do is share the specifics that pertain to their parts of the project with each of those individuals.

Oftentimes, the whole project gets thrown into the work of a functional area in the business without much thought about who really will be responsible for it. In that case, you'll have to take more time to communicate all the specifics about the deliverables to everyone who's involved in that functional area.

Finally, in the worst case, there are no resources dedicated to maintaining the project deliverables. As project manager, you can complain about this, but there's a chance that no one will listen. In that case, you have to make the difficult decision to walk away. Be certain that your documentation is archived completely and that the stakeholders have been notified formally about the project ending and the location of the final deliverable. Then, move on.

What If I Skip This Step?

Projects are hard work and it's so tempting to let your guard down as the end approaches. People begin to relax a little and generally feel pretty good about themselves and each other. And it's tempting to gloss over formal ending procedures. But not ending a project well costs the business in several ways:

- Multiple people doing similar work: If the hand-off to the business is not clear, chances are good that people on the project team will continue working on the project, as will the stakeholders. Redundant work is very expensive and unnecessary. Unclear roles also create conflict very quickly.
- The cost to you is that you're working on too many things: If you've done a good job on the project and you've built a lot of trust with the stakeholders, it will be natural for them to call you for help even after the project ends. At first, it might feel good to be so valuable, but eventually you'll be embroiled in the copious responsibilities of a new assignment and you'll find that the recurring calls and questions are preventing you from getting your current work done.

Lurking Landmines

- *The project's final product or service has been delivered and the transition completed, but your client hasn't paid your earlier invoices.* This is a tricky situation. Let's say your client is a little behind on payment for work you've delivered and invoiced. Do you hold off the project transition and implementation until all earlier invoices have been paid? This is a situation that demands you speak frankly with your sponsor to find out what's holding up payments. In worst-case scenarios, you may have to state clearly that you will deliver the final pieces only when the outstanding invoices have been paid. That's a very bad situation to be in and taking that tack can create conflict, but sometimes it's your only recourse.
- *Sponsorship changes at the last minute.* If there is a reorganization late in the project, it can be devastating to your plans for project completion because new sponsors almost always have new requirements. If possible, get sign-off on the project product or service deliverables from the original sponsor before he or she leaves. Meet as soon as you can

with the new sponsor to review the project status. Make it clear that his or her support and sponsorship are critical to a successful completion.

Step 9 Checklist

✓ Be sure that you have built and shared all the documentation recommended in Steps 2, 3, and 4—business and project objectives, scope diagram, risk assessments, statement of constraints, and role definitions.

✓ Proceed more formally than you feel you should. Keep the project plan tight all the way through the transition to the business area.

✓ Involve the sponsors constantly as your project moves into the business area.

The Next Step

The final step in managing your project is learning from it. Having the discipline to do a post-project review will strengthen your project management skills and prepare you for even more success in future projects.

NOTES

STEP **9**

Follow Up to Learn Lessons

When the project is over you'd like to think about something else. Your entire team feels the same way and, in the hallway, stakeholders are avoiding eye contact with you. The last thing anyone wants to do is revisit the project and its missteps, bad choices, delays, conflicts, and weak outcomes. No one even wants to bring up the good parts—the happy surprises, the mended relationships, the amazing saves, or the deep friendships. But there is gold in all those hills, and the last step in successful project management is to find it and mine it.

Years ago, I was the leader of the IT subproject on a large project that was highly time constrained and very visible to our external customers. It was politically charged, and we dared not fail. The end product was a two-week customer event at pre-Olympic trials. Among other things, we had to deliver sports tickets, hotel rooms, meals, shows, and transportation. From the perspectives of sponsor and customer, the project was a success. From the teams' perspective, there were some big problems. It was in this project that I first saw the value of holding a post-project review.

When BB opened

the diner door and let in the three little pigs, everyone at the counter turned around, surprised to see this group come in and sit together as friends.

As the four ate their pancakes, they talked about all they'd been through together.

"You know, fellas, my family got into the huff-and-puff business when they passed that law about not eating chickens," BB told them. "Chickens were our bread and butter, and they took that away. Knocking down your houses wasn't personal—it was survival."

The pigs told BB about their three strategies for building shelters. Speedy said he'd moved too fast because he couldn't believe BB would be coming after him. In his hurry, he veered off course and slapped together a house that didn't meet his original goals. And then he got distracted by the sticks and the music he could make with them.

Goldy admitted that he'd made a few mistakes of his own. He moved too slowly, looking for the cheapest way to get something done. He'd found free straw—but not enough of it. It was too late to get more straw, so he'd used scraps of trash to finish his house. His original plan wasn't solid, and the makeshift result was far from stable.

Demmy was glad his house had saved them, but he said he knew there were flaws in his approach, too. He'd been so caught up in building the perfect house that he was paralyzed by planning. When he finally began to build, it was almost too late. And the roof was such an afterthought that without his brothers' help, it never would have held.

So, they'd all learned some lessons:

- Balance speed, cost, and quality for any project because focusing on just one will generally make you fail.
- A little planning and "what-if" thinking really helps.
- Three pigs are better than one.
- Collaboration is the path to success. Both BB and the three little Oinks had a problem. And when they listened calmly to one another, they found a way to solve it so everyone was satisfied.

Emotions were high during the project. One project manager oversaw project leaders heading six different subprojects, and everyone lived in different states. For all of us, our project responsibilities (presented to us as a "great career opportunity") were in addition to our regular jobs.

As the project started to hit snags, strategic alliances began to develop, roles became murky, and at least one person didn't pull his weight. We all grew angry about the shirking, and a few of us went to the project manager to ask that he do something about the nonperformer. He did nothing, and if you'd asked me then what the major project problem was, I'd have told you we had a weak and ineffective project manager because he wouldn't control the team.

Three months after the project ended, we met again as a team. Prior to that meeting, we each put our thoughts about the project on paper and emailed them to the project manager. Although I don't remember ever seeing the results of those emails, it forced me to take a careful look back at the project. From three months out, my opinion had changed. To my surprise, I realized that when the project manager refused to solve our team issues, he helped the project tremendously. If we had had to depend on him to monitor and manage our relationships, we never would have met our project goals. Instead, we were forced to take care of the shirking problem ourselves, often picking up the dropped work. In fixing the problem, we kept the project on track. I don't know if the project manager did this on purpose, or if it was his natural style and just lucky for this project. Either way, it worked. It was a lesson that I try to remember on my own projects because I tend toward micromanaging.

What's meaningful about that story here in Step 10 is that I would not have learned that lesson if I hadn't taken the opportunity to reflect on the completed project from the vantage point of a little time and distance. What nuggets can you learn from your previous project experiences? Learning theory and knowledge management research have shown that people can't learn on a macro level while they're in an experience. Learning occurs after the experience is over when they think about what happened.

It's tough to get people to participate in a review unless your company has a pertinent and enforceable policy. Even if no one else is able to participate, give yourself an hour to think through the lessons learned on the project. Ask yourself these questions:

1. What went well on this project? What would I do again on future projects?
2. What did not go well on this project? What would I change on future projects?

Simply becoming conscious of what did or didn't work will improve your ability to manage projects successfully.

We are at the last phase of our Dare to Properly Manage Resources Model. In this step, we focus on **Review.** You'll learn about both the value of and processes for facilitating a post-project review. If possible, find a quick and simple way for all participants to share their thoughts about the project. Obviously, you have to have a pretty tough skin to ask for feedback, but it's well worth it. If they won't participate, do a post-project review yourself. Learning still will occur.

Time to Complete This Step

A post-project review can take anywhere from 30 minutes to two days. If you're doing it by yourself, you can grab a cup of coffee and think about the project for 30 minutes or so. If you're doing the review through a facilitated session with a large number of stakeholders, it can take from one to two days, depending on the techniques used and the number of participants.

Stakeholders

If you can get all of your project's stakeholders to participate in a post-project review, it's a tremendous gain for everyone. All of the perspectives that will be represented at the table offer a rare 360-degree view of the project. The sponsors will see the project from a different viewpoint than the stakeholders and the project team members. And they'll all see it somewhat differently from the way you see it.

Questions to Ask

Questions can be simple and wide ranging or pointed and more deeply revelatory. On the simpler side are these two questions:

1. What went well on this project? What would I do again on future projects?
2. What did not go well on this project? What would I change on future projects?

These questions are open-ended and can be used for sponsors and stakeholders who won't be able to commit much time to a review. The questions are also excellent for leading a discussion face-to-face with the project team. By leaving the discussion more open, you'll get very different responses from different people, and those responses will trigger great learning.

For a more pointed review of the specific aspects of your project, use the questions in tool 10.1 with members of the project team and with stakeholders who were more involved in the work. If the project was larger and more complex, thus meriting more review time and investment, use these more probing queries. These questions also may produce better responses than the more open questions when the review is not going to be done face-to-face.

Project Manager's Toolkit: Techniques for Post-Project Reviews

Companies serious about growing project management competence keep the project lessons learned in a searchable file. Keeping a knowledge base of these data requires a commitment of time, database expertise, and business intelligence expertise. Investing in this type of knowledge base provides the company with a way to learn from actual results. These results can be used to jump-start new project teams, which improves project results dramatically. The project management office is a good place for this activity to be housed.

Example 10.1 lists some of my favorite learning nuggets from reviews I've done for clients. Use this list to jump-start your next project.

Depending on the size and risk of your project and the current time commitments of the people whose participation you'd like to engage in your review, choose among the following approaches when holding a post-project review:

♦ face-to-face versus virtual meetings via phone, webinar, or email

TOOL 10.1

Questions for a Thorough Review

1. How close to the scheduled completion date was the project actually finished?

2. What did we learn about scheduling that will help us on our next project?

3. How close to budget was the final project cost?

4. What did we learn about budgeting that will help us on our next project?

5. What did we learn about communication during the project?

6. At completion, did the project output meet client specifications without additional work?

7. What, if any, additional work was required?

8. What did we learn about writing specifications that will help us on our next project?

9. What did we learn about staffing that will help us on our next project?

10. What did we learn about managing conflict through negotiation on this project?

11. What did we learn about monitoring performance that will help us on our next project?

12. What did we learn about taking corrective action that will help us on our next project?

13. What technological advances were made on this project?

14. What tools and techniques were developed that will be useful on our next project?

15. What recommendations do we have for future research and development?

16. What lessons did we learn from our dealings with service organizations and outside vendors?

17. If we had the opportunity to redo the project, what would we do differently?

EXAMPLE 10.1

Sample Lessons Learned in Post-Project Reviews

1. You can never ask too many questions.

2. Trust your instincts.

3. The more you can help people focus on one task, the more velocity your project can maintain.

4. Hand-offs kill.

5. During times of trouble, more communication is better than less.

6. Without project management documentation and process, everyone depends on the project manager to answer all their questions and direct them. For small projects, you might be able to depend on a single person to keep all the project knowledge in his or her head, but for a medium-size to large project, it isn't feasible.

7. No project will be perfect.

8. No issue is insurmountable if you're creative enough.

9. Projects generally don't fail because the project definition is faulty or the project schedule is inadequate. Projects fail because people fail to communicate.

10. Investing in structured processes, rules of order, and roles to make your meetings effective is an important way to improve the odds of project success.

◆ discussions versus individual surveys

◆ mixed groups versus subteams focused on one aspect or activity of the project.

In planning your review, remember that the more diverse the groups involved, the better the results—but there's also more risk of conflict. Think about how you'll gather the lessons learned and how you'll share the results after you've synthesized everyone's responses.

How Long Should You Wait Before Conducting a Review?

I've found that post-project reviews are most effective when they occur between three and six months after a project is completed. Such a pause ensures that the project is really over, but isn't so long that people really can't recall details. The trick to successfully timing the review is to get far enough from the day-to-day action of the project that your participants have a more holistic view of it, but not to wait so long that the details are gone.

What Can You Do at the Post-Project Review?

If you have the luxury of face-to-face meetings, you can do the post-project review and celebrate the successful completion of the project in the same event, and you should do both. This works well for very large projects that were geographically dispersed. It may take a few months to get the relevant players together. The added benefit is that a "celebration" tends to trigger better participation than a more serious-sounding "post-project review."

If possible, find as a facilitator someone who wasn't directly involved in the project. (It's also good if meeting participants don't work for the facilitator.) If it's impossible to find someone to facilitate, the project manager may end up playing that role.

In either case, simply leading an open discussion without a structured facilitation approach is generally **not** an effective and safe way to gather lessons learned. There can be a lot of charged-up feelings waiting to explode, and there may be people who don't feel their views are important to anyone else. Using one of the facilitation techniques described below will promote equal participation. In addition, these facilitation techniques will be different enough from the normal project meetings that participants will be unable to fall into their old communication patterns. This tends to make the discussions not only more safe, but also more open. Consider using one, some, or all the following techniques.

Learning History

Use this technique where there were some major conflicts on the project that have never been discussed fully. This technique offers a safe way for participants to reveal the emotional baggage they carried from the project, and it helps keep them from lugging that

TOOL 10.2

Steps of the Learning History Review Process

1. Ask everyone to type up a one-page description of the project, viewed from their perspective. Ask them to tell a story of something that happened that they believe is indicative of things that happened throughout the project. Each person will have an individual story that's extremely meaningful to them. In some cases, the stories involve big wins, but most often the stories will focus on things that didn't go well for the writers.

2. Ask each participant to email her or his one-page "learning history" to the facilitator. Explain that copies will be made for other participants.

3. At the group meeting, the facilitator hands out copies of the stories so that all attendees can read along as each person reads his or her story aloud.

4. After each story, other participants are invited to ask clarifying questions about the story.

5. When the questions have been discussed, the facilitator asks the group to brainstorm lessons, and then lists them on a flipchart. This same process is repeated for each story. When all stories have been read and discussed, review the lessons listed on the flipchart.

baggage to future projects. The technique comes from the field of knowledge management, and the process is described in tool 10.2.

A learning history is a stunningly effective technique for revealing feelings. People write and then read stories about the project with greater honesty than they normally would share in a forthright discussion format. Good facilitation is critical, and it may be important to lay out some ground rules at the beginning. No person may be victimized or ridiculed for his or her honesty. The discussion that follows each reading must be controlled so that it doesn't become a debate over the accuracy of the story. Remind the participants that what each story reveals is the writer's perception of reality, and it may or may not be the same reality others perceived.

After everyone has had a turn, review the flipchart list of lessons learned, removing and combining them as the group suggests to make a concise list that can be shared with others.

STEP 10

Sticky-Note Analysis

Use this technique when a great deal of conflict still exists among the participants. This approach will allow differing opinions to be expressed anonymously. The technique works well as an opening facilitation approach when followed by a different technique that drills down further into the specifics of the conflict, like the learning history technique.

Tool 10.3 describes the process for sticky-note analysis. As with the learning histories, the products of this review are documented lessons learned.

Appreciative Inquiry

Use this technique when the project team has worked really hard and been very successful but hasn't been recognized for their effort or the project outcome. Often, teams that have a major disaster and then recover are recognized more than teams that stayed the course and finished well without a major incident.

There are many resources available—especially on the web—to help you facilitate this technique. Here we'll use a basic approach, described in tool 10.4. The idea behind appreciative inquiry is to look for the positive rather than the negative aspects of a successful project. In identifying what factors supported and promoted specific and overarching successes, participants discover how to repeat these successes in the future. The energy of discussing and learning from the positives is a wonderful way to learn from each other and celebrate project completion.

Web Surveys

Use web-based surveys when you need to gather lessons learned without revealing respondents' identities or when respondents are dispersed geographically and unlikely to come back together. There are inexpensive ways to do web surveys that make it easy to gather and summarize information, including www.surveymonkey.com or

TOOL 10.3

Sticky-Note Analysis Review Process

Use these questions for this review technique:

- What went well on this project? What would I do again on future projects?
- What did not go well on this project? What would I change on future projects?

Listed below are the steps to follow in facilitating this review.

1. Provide pencils and a pad of same-color sticky-notes to all participants.

2. Ask each participant to answer the questions about *what went well* on the project by writing one thought per note. Allow enough time for participants to keep writing until they've answered the questions as fully as they can. What usually works for this is to wait until about 80 percent of them are obviously finished and then announce that 30 seconds of writing time remains. Tell them to place their piles of notes in front of them.

3. Repeat step 2 with the questions pertaining to *what didn't go well.*

4. Group the participants into teams of three to five people. Assign each group a specific area on the wall, and ask them to put all their individual sticky-notes up on that area *without speaking to anyone else* while they do it. This will take only a couple of minutes. They should remain at the wall until they're finished placing their notes.

5. With the same team of people, before the team members have time to start looking at each other's notes, ask them to begin—again *silently*—grouping similar notes together. Tell them they may move any note they wish (not just their own). At this point, people lose track of who wrote what, and that maintains the anonymous feel of this exercise.

6. Gently reinforce the silence of this part of the exercise, and let the grouping continue until about half the teams seem to be finished. This normally takes 5–10 minutes.

7. Ask participants to continue grouping for two more minutes, now letting them talk to each other. This enables them to clarify the groupings they've already made.

8. Give each team one pad of notes of a different color. Ask the teams to use these notes to label each grouping.

9. Ask each team to tell the entire group how they labeled their note groups and to read some of the details on the notes. When a team is done explaining its results, ask the group to brainstorm and share lessons learned from that team's work and to list the lessons learned on flipchart paper.

10. Conclude this review by asking each person to share what he or she thinks is the most important lesson. Record this by putting a checkmark next to that lesson on the flipchart page. This can also be typed up and distributed electronically to the participants and to future project managers.

TOOL 10.4

Appreciative Inquiry Review Process

Depending on the size of the group, break into teams of three to five people. Appoint a leader for each team, using strange criteria like "the person with the oldest car." Explain that each team will follow this process:

1. The leader will ask each team member to share a story about a success on the project. Each person will take up to five minutes to tell the story. The others can ask questions.

2. Then the leader will ask the team to revisit each of the stories and define what it was that caused the success. Some examples might be *good communication*, *strong leadership*, *innovation*, and so forth. The team leader will document these causes on a flipchart or on note paper. Many stories will have similar causes.

3. The teams will be brought back into one large group, and the team leaders will share their lists while the facilitator writes the items of all the lists on a flipchart.

4. The group will discuss what steps to take on future projects to ensure that similar successes occur. In other words, they'll describe how to create an environment for success.

---

www.freeonlinesurveys.com. Use these tools to create one of the following:

◆ **Simple survey** (sometimes called a "smile sheet"): In this type of survey, you list the issues on the project that you believe will be important to the participants. Then, you ask each participant to rate the importance of the issue numerically—for example, from *Not Important* (1) to *Extremely Important* (5). Using a numeric ranking approach makes it easy to summarize large amounts of data. However, if you find out that an issue has been rated low, it's difficult to understand why people feel that way. Tool 10.5 is a sample survey of this kind.

◆ **Emotion-based survey:** In this type of survey, participants are asked how they feel about the project success, and then asked why they feel that way. Through this approach, participants generate the issues they feel merit discussion. By starting with emotions, people tend to list the things that really affected them. The strength of the emotion is used to prioritize which issues really affected the project team. This type of survey is more difficult to construct and summarize using simple survey tools, but web versions are available (for example, see the Clarity survey at www.russellmartin.com). Tool 10.6 offers some typical items from a survey of this type.

Nominal Group Technique

This technique leverages the power of email to gather information. You can use it when you don't have time to meet with everyone or they don't have time to meet with you. Use this technique to gather anonymous data through email. It works best when you start

TOOL 10.5

Simple Survey

Instructions: For each of the following project factors, rate its quality by circling the appropriate number on the scale. If a factor was not pertinent to the project, circle "not applicable." Add any comments you believe will be helpful in explaining your rating.

1. Planned schedule
   Comments:
   1 2 3 4 5 6 7 8 9 10   NOT APPLICABLE
   LOWEST   HIGHEST

2. Actual time used
   Comments:
   1 2 3 4 5 6 7 8 9 10   NOT APPLICABLE
   LOWEST   HIGHEST

3. Planned budget
   Comments:
   1 2 3 4 5 6 7 8 9 10   NOT APPLICABLE
   LOWEST   HIGHEST

4. Actual budget used
   Comments:
   1 2 3 4 5 6 7 8 9 10   NOT APPLICABLE
   LOWEST   HIGHEST

5. Requirements clearly defined
   Comments:
   1 2 3 4 5 6 7 8 9 10   NOT APPLICABLE
   LOWEST   HIGHEST

continued on next page

6. Project staffing and roles
   Comments:
   1 2 3 4 5 6 7 8 9 10
   LOWEST · HIGHEST
   NOT APPLICABLE

7. Project communication
   Comments:
   1 2 3 4 5 6 7 8 9 10
   LOWEST · HIGHEST
   NOT APPLICABLE

8. Implemented technology
   Comments:
   1 2 3 4 5 6 7 8 9 10
   LOWEST · HIGHEST
   NOT APPLICABLE

9. Monitoring of project progress
   Comments:
   1 2 3 4 5 6 7 8 9 10
   LOWEST · HIGHEST
   NOT APPLICABLE

10. Tools and techniques used
    Comments:
    1 2 3 4 5 6 7 8 9 10
    LOWEST · HIGHEST
    NOT APPLICABLE

11. Research and development
    when needed
    Comments:
    1 2 3 4 5 6 7 8 9 10
    LOWEST · HIGHEST
    NOT APPLICABLE

12. Vendor involvement
    Comments:
    1 2 3 4 5 6 7 8 9 10
    LOWEST · HIGHEST
    NOT APPLICABLE

13. Internal service organization
    involvement
    Comments:
    1 2 3 4 5 6 7 8 9 10
    LOWEST · HIGHEST
    NOT APPLICABLE

TOOL 10.6

Emotion-Based Survey Items

1. Describe the problems experienced on the project by entering on this line the emotion you felt: _____.

2. Rank the intensity of that emotion (1 = low, 10 = high): _____.

3. What factors contributed to your feelings about the problems?

4. Describe the successes experienced on the project by entering on this line the emotion you felt: _____.

5. Rank the intensity of that emotion (1 = low, 10 = high): _____.

6. What factors contributed to your feelings about the successes?

with open-ended instructions. Here are two that I use, depending on the project:

- ◆ List the 10 things you would do differently if we repeated this project.
- ◆ List the 10 things you would do the same way if we repeated this project.

Tool 10.7 describes the nominal group process using email. The technique also can be used in a group setting if the facilitator en-

TOOL 10.7

Nominal Group Technique Using Email

To make this process easier to understand, we'll use an example. Let's say you're doing a review of a project on which there was an issue with the initial task estimate. Here are the steps you follow to use email with the nominal group technique:

1. Email all the stakeholders the following message, being careful to phrase the controversial project issue in neutral terms: "We will be using an email facilitation technique to share our thoughts around the initial task estimate. Please rate the impact of this issue by responding with a number between 1 (low impact) and 6 (high impact). Email me your choice by [*insert date*]. Your response will be kept completely anonymous."

2. Tally the responses you receive and report the outcome to each participant with this email: "Thanks for your participation. Here are the results of my initial data gathering: the average response was 3.5, the highest response was 5, and the lowest response was 2. I would like you to participate in a second round by sharing with me your rating (you may change it or keep it the same), and three reasons why you chose that number. If you are contributing for the first time, simply let me know your rating (1 = low impact; 6 = high impact) for this issue and give me your three reasons for your choice."

3. Again tally the choices and summarize the reasons respondents submit. Send the tally and summary back to each individual.

4. Continue this process until you have consensus (which will probably not occur over email) or you can see that two definitive alternatives are polarizing participants. Bring people together physically to discuss the final two alternatives and move to consensus.

Warning: If you do too many iterations of this technique, the results tend to polarize. Try to stop before it has become too obvious to people that lines are being drawn.

STEP 10

forces strict rules for participation. Specifically, all participants *must* respond clockwise from the facilitator, and must speak for a defined period of time (for example, five minutes). No one else may talk during another person's time.

Communication

As early as possible in the project, remind stakeholders that you'll be inviting them to take part in a post-project review after the completion of the project. This will help them think as they go and notice project issues, constraints, successes, and lessons they can share with others later.

The lessons learned need to be summarized and captured. Revisit your initial communication plan and send the summarized lessons to the same list of stakeholders. The sponsor needs a very macro-level look at the results, whereas the project team members need a more detailed summary of the lessons so they can make the most of them in subsequent projects. At a minimum, remember to make sure that all participants receive summarized lessons. There's nothing worse than investing your time in one of these reviews and then never hearing anything from it after the fact.

What If I Skip This Step?

Most people skip the post-project review—and that may explain why most companies are struggling more than ever with their projects. If you don't learn from your mistakes, you're destined to repeat them. You alone choose whether to prioritize the time to learn. Even if no one else wants to do the project review with you, there is tremendous value in taking as much time as you can squeeze out of your day to think through the project and harvest lessons for subsequent work.

Lurking Landmine

◆ *Nobody wants to come to your review meeting or complete your survey.* There's a lot of resistance to reviews because many people fear that the meetings turn into blame sessions. Try to find a way that's less time consuming and completely safe to encourage people's participation. Even if you can get them to send you only a simple email with "what went well, what didn't go so well," you'll learn something. Ask for their help—people generally like to respond to that. Ask more than once so they know it's important to you.

Step 10 Checklist

✓ Remind people during the project that there will be a post-project review approximately three months after project completion.

✓ Document the lessons learned and share them with others.

NOTES

STEP **10**

CONCLUSION

In reading my 10 steps to project management, I hope you've picked up many new tips and techniques and adapted the way you approach your projects, aiming for flexible structure instead of total control.

While what you've learned is fresh, take some time to make notes of the lessons from each step. Use worksheet C.1 to record your notes and refer to it before you start your next project. When you acquire any new skills, it's a good idea to pick no more than three to try out at any given time. As those become second nature, pick another three skills.

What are the top three ideas you plan to implement on your projects after investing your time reading this book?

1. _____

2. _____

3. _____

The struggles you encounter on your projects are not unique. Everywhere, people are worried about their ability to manage the growing number of projects for which they're responsible. Making the time and bearing the risk to stop, learn, and apply something new takes great courage.

Our Little Pigs share a universally understood project challenge. Their tale emerges in other cultures with different contexts and villains, but the same results. "The Three Little Javelinas" by Susan Lowell and "The Three Little Hawaiian Pigs and the Magic Shark" by Donivee Martin Laird are cultural variations on the classic theme. I wonder whether Speedy, Goldy, and Demmy really could change their ways, or if they'd just repeat the same mistakes over and over. They've had plenty to learn, but will they? Will you?

WORKSHEET C.1

Lessons Learned in the *10 Steps of Successful Project Management*

Instructions: Think about what you've learned in reading this book. In the space following each of the steps below, make notes to use as a checklist and reminder when you start your next project.

Step 1: Decide If You Have a Real Project to Manage

_____

_____

Step 2: Prove Your Project Is Worth Your Time

_____

_____

Step 3: Manage Scope Creep

_____

Step 4: Identify, Rate, and Manage Risks

_____

Step 5: Collaborate Successfully

_____

Step 6: Gather Your Team and Make a Schedule

_____

Step 7: Adjust Your Schedule

_____

Step 8: Embrace the Natural Chaos of People

_____

Step 9: Know When You're Done

_____

Step 10: Follow Up to Learn Lessons

_____

At the beginning of this book, you learned about my fascination with the three pigs and their lessons for us regarding project management. To finish the way I started, I searched the web to see if anyone did an article or story about the pigs after the story. Instead I found this bizarre report from Reuters:

> *BEIJING*—Chinese scientists have successfully bred partially green fluorescent pigs, which they hope will boost stem cell research, Xinhua news agency said. Scientists say they have successfully bred three pigs [that] glow fluorescent green in the dark, marking a breakthrough in stem cell research (December 28, 2006).

How would this surprise have affected our three pigs' building project? Would the fluorescent color have made it easier for BB Wolf to spot them? Or would glowing green pigs have scared him away? Turns out even the fairy tale world of the three pigs may be changed by amazing reality.

Every "next project" will bring with it new challenges. No matter how much we hope for the perfect project—no delays, no surprises, no changes, no failures—that project eludes us. As hard as we try to predict and prepare for the future, it surprises us. At the heart of it all we are best prepared when we practice flexible structure—at all times, have a plan; but at all times, be prepared to adapt that plan as changes demand it.

I'm going to close here with just one more pig story. Alan Colquit told me this story, and it's germane to our work as project managers. Once upon a time, there was a group of pigs that lived on an island where food was running out. The pigs held an emergency meeting and, after much deliberation, decided to use what remained of their food to build a boat and sail off in search of provisions. None of them had ever been across the water, but they felt they were choosing probable death over certain death, so off they went. Your role as project manager is similar to the role of the pig who captained that boat—you moved the pigs through great uncertainty. And your most important work? To keep the pigs from eating the boat.

A P P E N D I X

Teaching Others These 10 Steps

When I read a book that makes a strong impression on me, I can't wait to share it with my staff. It usually takes a lot of time to choose and organize the points to share and figure out the best way to do it. In this appendix, I'd like to give you some guidelines for sharing this material with your teams so you can do it with little effort.

Target Audience: Anyone who has to manage projects, especially people who don't call themselves "project managers"

Participant Preparation: Each person being trained should choose one of the projects they are working on when the class is held as a test case. As they work through each step, they'll learn and understand more if they apply the lessons to that sample project.

Your Preparation to Teach the Class:
- Summarize key bullet points for each step and create a PowerPoint presentation for your use in class.
- Build the student guide from a print version of your Power-Point presentation and print out from the CD-ROM a copy of each tool, worksheet, figure, and example you'd like to share.

Agendas: I recommend approaching this information sharing more as a study group than as a training class, but either context will work. For a quick overview, consider the one-hour agenda offered in table A.1. If you can dedicate more time, your colleagues will gain more expertise by going through all 10 steps in a two-day session (table A.2). A third option is to hold six 90-minute sessions, either live or through a synchronous webinar when colleagues are geographically dispersed. For more information about webinars and for free webinars you can attend to see how it's done, check out www.elluminate.com or www.webx.com. Table A.3 presents a six-session agenda.

Signature Mini-Project

1. Break your group into teams of three to five people and explain that each group will work as a project team.
2. Write the following project objective on a flipchart or whiteboard: *Your project is to get signatures from everyone in the room in five minutes.*
3. Give the teams three minutes to strategize. Don't let them start until the three minutes are up.
4. Call "Go!" Let the teams gather signatures for five minutes.
5. Open a discussion about what went well, what didn't go well, and how those aspects do or don't resemble their real-world projects.

Variation: To make this exercise work in a context that's not face-to-face (for example, in a webinar format), use the following project objective: *Your project is to get the middle name of each participant in five minutes.*

TABLE A.1

One-Hour Session

This agenda focuses primarily on Steps 2, 3, and 4. The idea is to introduce the four-phase management model (define, plan, manage, review) but spend most of the hour learning and practicing how to start a project well.

Time to Complete	Topic	Participant Practice
15 minutes	Open the session and introduce project management	Do the Signature Mini-Project
5 minutes	Step 1: Is it a project or a task?	
10 minutes	Step 2: What are the business objectives?	Write a set of objectives for your project
20 minutes	Step 3: What are the project objectives and scope?	Draw a quick scope diagram for your project
5 minutes	Step 4: What are the project's risks and constraints?	Do a quick-and-dirty risk assessment for your project
5 minutes	Step 6: How should the tasks and resources be scheduled?	

TABLE A.2

Two-Day Session

This agenda addresses all 10 steps. Each participant applies the steps to a project she or he is working on in the real world. If that isn't feasible, ask participants to work on a project of your choosing. Getting hands-on experience with the steps is the most important aspect of this training.

Time to Complete	Topic	Participant Practice
Day 1 30 minutes	Open the meeting and introduce project management	◆ Do the Signature Mini-Project
1 hour	Step 1: Is it a project or a task?	◆ Share something on your to-do list that has been on there forever and probably is a project rather than a task ◆ Discuss how you might manage projects using your office software
1 hour	Step 2: What are the business objectives?	◆ List all the business objectives for your project ◆ Share these objectives with one other person and improve your list
3 hours	Step 3: What are the project objectives and scope?	◆ Draw a scope diagram for your project; share it with others and improve it ◆ Build a complete list of project objectives; share the objectives with others and improve your list
2 hours	Step 4: What are the project's risks and constraints?	◆ Perform a quick-and-dirty risk assessment • Complete a risk scenario document for your project • Build a constraints diagram

Day 2		
1 hour	Step 5: What leadership skills do project managers need?	◆ Complete worksheet 5.1 to assess your project management leadership ability ◆ Discuss what leadership tasks are most difficult to perform ◆ Discuss coaching and delegation challenges, using real-life examples
2 hours	Step 6: How should the tasks and resources be scheduled?	◆ Build a critical path diagram for your project ◆ Estimate and assign resources
1 hour	Step 7: What kind of tracking log is best when the project is small or medium-size?	◆ Convert the critical path diagram you created for your project into a project tracking spreadsheet that tracks by dates instead of tasks
1 hour	Step 8: How can conflict and chaos be managed?	◆ Discuss real conflict situations and negotiations that have occurred on other projects ◆ Build checklists for success
1 hour	Step 9: How do you know when the project is finished?	◆ Create a checklist of ending criteria for your project
1 hour	Step 10: How can you identify the lessons you've learned when a project has gone well?	◆ Use the appreciative inquiry review technique with your group, focusing on previous projects ◆ Gather lessons learned to use for future projects

Note: If you have leadership training available at your company, you can spend less time on Step 5 if you simply discuss the training that's already occurred.

TABLE A.3

Six-Session Meeting or Webinar

This agenda addresses all 10 steps. Between sessions, each participant will apply to her or his own projects the techniques learned in the preceding sessions.

Time to Complete	Topic	Participant Practice
Session 1 15 minutes	Introduce project management	• Do the Signature Mini-Project (use the optional project objective if this session is a webinar)
15 minutes	Step 1: Is it a project or a task?	• Share something on your to-do list that has been on there forever and probably is a project rather than a task
1 hour	Step 2: What are the business objectives?	• List all the business objectives for your project; share these objectives with one other person and improve your list
Session 2 1.5 hours	Step 3: What are the project objectives and scope?	• Draw a scope diagram for your project; share it with others and improve it • Build a complete list of project objectives; share the objectives with others and improve your list
Session 3 1 hour	Step 4: What are the project's risks and constraints?	• Perform a quick-and-dirty risk assessment • Complete a risk scenario document for your project • Build a constraints diagram

Time	Step	Activities
30 minutes	Step 5: What leadership skills do project managers need?	◆ Complete worksheet 5.1 to assess your project management leadership ability ◆ Discuss what leadership tasks are most difficult to perform
Session 4 1.5 hours	Step 6: How should the tasks and resources be scheduled?	◆ Build a critical path diagram for your project
Session 5 1 hour	Step 7: What kind of tracking log is best when the project is small or medium-size?	◆ Convert the critical path diagram you created for your project into a project tracking spreadsheet that tracks by dates instead of tasks
30 minutes	Step 8: How can conflict and chaos be managed?	◆ Discuss real conflict situations and negotiations that have occurred on other projects ◆ Build checklists for success
Session 6 30 minutes	Step 9: How do you know when the project is finished?	◆ Create a checklist of ending criteria for your project
1 hour	Step 10: How can you identify the lessons you've learned when a project has gone well?	◆ Use the appreciative inquiry review technique with your group, focusing on previous projects ◆ Gather lessons learned to use for future projects

Note: If you have leadership training available at your company, you can spend less time on Step 5 by simply discussing the training that's already occurred.

R E S O U R C E S

Resource: David Allen
Description: Expert on personal productivity and time management
Contact information: http://www.davidco.com

Resource: ASK Magazine
Description: Excellent online magazine from NASA, with project management stories and lessons learned
Contact information: http://appel.nasa.gov/ask

Resource: Michael Ayers and the Commonwealth Practice
Description: Has done research on resistance and leadership
Contact information: http://www.thecommonwealthpractice.com

Resource: Fred Brooks
Description: Software engineer and computer scientist; author of *The Mythical Man-Month,* which described his experience developing the IBM OS/360
Contact information: http://en.wikipedia.org/wiki/Fred_Brooks (for information about Brooks)

Resource: DISC literature
Description: My favorite DISC books include Julie Straw and Alison Brown Cerier's *The 4-Dimensional Manager: DISC Strategies for Managing Different People in the Best Ways* (San Francisco: Berrett-Koehler, 2002); and Tom Richey with Ron Axelrod's *I'm Stuck, You're Stuck: Break Through to Better Work Relationships and Results by Discovering Your DISC Behavioral Style* (San Francisco: Berrett-Koehler, 2002).
Contact information: http://www.russellmartin.com (to order profiles and books)

Resource: Randy Englund
Description: Co-author, with Robert J. Graham, *Creating an Environment for Successful Projects* (2003); with Robert J. Graham and Paul C. Dinsmore, *Creating the Project Office: a Managers Guide to Leading Organizational Change* (2003); and, with Alfonso Bucero, *Project Sponsorship: Achieving Management Commitment for Project Success* (2006) (all published by Jossey-Bass)
Contact information: http://home.pacbell.net/muellmar/index_picture.htm

Resource: *Harvard Business Review*
Description: journal published the classic article "Who's Got the Monkey?"
Contact information: http://harvardbusinessonline.hbsp.harvard.edu

Resource: Jim Highsmith
Description: Author of *Agile Project Management: Creating Innovative Products* (Boston: Addison-Wesley Professional, 2004)
Contact information: http://www.adaptivesd.com/

Resource: Guy Kawasaki
Description: Author of *Selling the Dream* (New York: Collins, 1992), and, with Michele Moreno, *Rules for Revolutionaries: The Capitalist Manifesto for Creating and Marketing New Products and Services* (New York: Harper Business, 2000)
Contact information: http://www.guykawasaki.com

Resource: Joan Knutson
Description: Project management guru; author or editor of many books, including *Project Management for Business Professionals: A Comprehensive Guide* (New York: Wiley, 2001)
Contact information: http://www.joanknutson.com/

Resource: The Liars Club
Description: David N. Ford and John Sterman's study focusing on why project managers lie about status and the cost of lying
Contact information: http://web.mit.edu/jsterman/www/Liar%27s_club.html

Resource: Michael Mah
Description: Author, speaker, consultant, and brilliant thinker; has done great work with metrics and project monitoring
Contact information: http://www.qsma.com/about_speaking.html

Resource: Glenn Parker
Description: Author of great books on teams and communication
Contact information: http://www.glennparker.com

Resource: Lou Russell
Description: Author of *The Accelerated Learning Fieldbook* (New York: Pfeiffer, 1999); *Project Management for Trainers* (Alexandria, VA: ASTD Press, 2000); with Jeff Feldman, *IT Leadership Alchemy* (New York: Prentice Hall, 2002); *Leadership Training* (Alexandria, VA: ASTD Press, 2003); and *Training Triage: Performance-Based Solutions amid Chaos, Confusion, and Change* (Alexandria, VA: ASTD Press, 2005)
Contact information: http://www.russellmartin.com

Resource: Bill Shackelford

Description: Author of *Project Managing E-Learning* (Alexandria, VA: ASTD Press, 2002)

Contact information: http://www.billshackelford.com

Resource: Bruce Tuckman

Description: Producer of original research on the Form, Storm, Norm, Perform team model

Source information: Tuckman, Bruce (1965), "Developmental Sequence in Small Groups," *Psychological Bulletin* 63: 384–99

Resource: William Ury

Description: Negotiation expert; author of *Getting Past No: Negotiating Your Way from Confrontation to Cooperation* (New York: Bantam Books, 1993)

Contact information: http://www.amazon.com

Resource: Villanova Continuing Studies

Description: Project management programs co-authored by Lou Russell and Joan Knutson

Contact information: http://www.villanovau.com/Content/Project Management.html

Resource: VNU Learning

Description: Online project management certificate program taught by Lou Russell

Contact information: http://home.learningtimes.net/vnucourses

I N D E X

L
learning history, 220–21

M
Manage (Dare Model phase): in
business cases, 207; definition,
13, 28–29; in risk management,
80; in schedules, 119, 131, 150,
154–57
management: benefits, 21–22; Edward Hoffman and, 2–3; success, 13–14; tasks and, 126
management software, 121–22
managers: assessment of leadership
abilities, 93–94; communication
and, 172–74; owners vs., 23–24;
questions for, 92–93, 121,
157–59, 166; return-on-investment and, 35; role of, 23, 28,
107–13; sponsors vs., 24–25,
171–72; stakeholders vs., 25–26;
teams, defining, 27, 30
Marston, William Moulton, 101
meetings, 111–13
multitasking, 17–18

N
NASA, 1–3
National Society of Professional Engineers, 1–2
negative feedback, 179–80,
184–87, 195–96
negotiation, 187–89
nominal group technique, 225,
227–28

O
objectives, 38–40, 42–43, 53–54,
63, 204
outputs, 50–53
owners, managers vs., 23–24

P
Plan (Dare Model phase): in business cases, 207; in communication, 193; definition, 12, 28–29;
in deliverables, 197; in schedules, 117, 129
plans: benefits, 21–22; building, 5,
7–8; clarifying, 31; creating, 10
see also schedules
post-project reviews: approaches
to, 218–19; communication and,
228; to increase competency, 9,
11; landmines, 228–29; questions and, 216–18; sample, 219;

skipping, 228; stakeholders and,
216; techniques for, 220–28;
time for, 216, 219–20; value of,
213, 215–16
priorities, 164–69
processes, projects vs., 20–21
Project Management Body of
Knowledge, 19–20
projects: adjustment of, 169–71;
benefits, 34; costs, 34–35;
defining worksheet, 19; definition, 19–20; ending, 197,
199–200, 205–12; processes vs.,
20–21; success, defining, 40,
43, 197, 199–200; tasks vs., 15,
18–19, 21, 30
project tracking spreadsheet,
144–47, 158, 160–64

Q
questions: in coaching, 110–11; for
managers, 92–93, 121, 157–59,
166, 216; for sponsors, 37–38,
120–21, 217; for stakeholders,
49–51, 70–71, 81–82, 99,
120–21, 181, 202, 216–18; for
teams, 217–18; vision, 96
quick-and-dirty risk assessments,
154–55

R
return-on-investment, 34–35
Review (Dare Model phase), 13, 29
reviews, post-project: approaches,
218–19; communication and,
228; to increase competency, 9,
11; landmines, 228–29; questions, 216–18; sample, 219;
skipping, 228; stakeholders and,
216; techniques for, 220–28;
time for, 216, 219–20; value of,
213, 215–16
risk management, 67–69, 72, 80,
86–87; see also risk scenarios
risk mitigation, 5–6
risks: definition, 67; documentation, 204; forecasting, 65, 67;
issues vs., 164–65; mitigation,
9–10; quick-and-dirty risk assessment, 72–76, 154–55; stakeholders and, 70
risk scenarios, 76–85, 126

S
schedules: adjustment of, 151,
153–54; advantages, 149; com-

Today's leaders must manage unprecedented rates of change and growth in a radically new and extraordinarily complex environment. With nearly 25 years of experience, **Lou Russell** has motivated and inspired some of the brightest business minds in the country. Russell is the CEO of Russell Martin & Associates, a consulting and training company focusing on improving planning, process, and performance. She is a consultant to companies, schools, and colleges; a popular author; and a dynamic and entertaining speaker who is considered a topic expert in the fields of training and performance, project management, and leadership. Russell's upbeat and humorous style enlightens and entertains as she offers practical insights for improving communication, teamwork, and leadership.

Russell's books include *The Accelerated Learning Fieldbook, Project Management for Trainers, IT Leadership Alchemy, Leadership Training,* and *Training Triage.* She is a frequent contributor to *Inside Indiana Business, Cutter Executive Reports,* and *Network World,* among other periodicals, and she publishes the monthly "Learning Flash" electronic newsletter. Russell has written project management programs for Villanova University and VNU Online Learning, as well as for many *Fortune* 1000 companies. Russell addresses national and international conferences, such as those of ASTD, Training, Training Directors Forum, Project Management Institute, Project World, and LotuSphere. She holds a computer science degree from Purdue University, where she taught database and programming classes, and a master's degree in instructional technology from Indiana University. Russell can be reached at 317.475.9311, lou@russellmartin.com.

Russell is married to Doug Martin and is mother to Kelly, Kristin, and Katherine. Her hobbies include soccer, running, teaching religious education, eating chocolate, introducing fun people to each other, and reading *People* magazine. She really isn't all that crazy about pigs.